Trade Union Women

Barbara M. Wertheimer
Anne H. Nelson

Published in cooperation with:
Trade Union Women's Studies
New York State School of
Industrial and Labor Relations
A Statutory College of the State University
Cornell University

The Praeger Special Studies program—
utilizing the most modern and efficient book
production techniques and a selective
worldwide distribution network—makes
available to the academic, government, and
business communities significant, timely
research in U.S. and international economic, social, and political development.

Trade Union Women.
A Study of Their Participation in New York City Locals

PRAEGER SPECIAL STUDIES IN U.S. ECONOMIC, SOCIAL, AND POLITICAL ISSUES

Praeger Publishers   New York   Washington   London

Library of Congress Cataloging in Publication Data

Wertheimer, Barbara M
  Trade union women.

  (Praeger special studies in U.S. economic, social,
and political issues)
  "Published in cooperation with Trade Union Women's
Studies, New York State School of Industrial and Labor
Relations...Cornell University."
  Includes bibliographical references and index.
  1. Women in trade-unions—New York (City) I. Nelson,
Anne H., joint author. II. Title.
HD6079.W47   331.88   74-32398
ISBN 0-275-05850-6

PRAEGER PUBLISHERS
111 Fourth Avenue, New York, N.Y. 10003, U.S.A.
5, Cromwell Place, London SW7 2JL, England

Published in the United States of America in 1975
by Praeger Publishers, Inc.

Printed in the United States of America

To the leaders, staff, and rank
and file members of the seven
unions who contributed to this
book.

In September 1972, the metropolitan office of the
New York State School of Industrial and Labor Relations,
Cornell University, was funded by the Ford Foundation to
study the barriers that keep working women from participating more fully in their labor union organizations. The
study grew out of several years' experience developing
courses for women unionists on subjects such as working
women and the law, women in the work force today, equal
employment problems, and women in American labor history.
The women participating in these courses, and those who
took part in day-long Cornell conferences for women union
leaders, staff, and activists, are among the pioneers in
a growing movement of union women devoted to building the
role of women in the day-to-day operations of their labor
unions.

Although activity in New York City came early, union
women across the country are now astir. In March 1974, a
new national organization was born: the Coalition of Labor Union Women, known as CLUW. Its mission is to unite
women unionists to work together in achieving these goals
of special concern to women workers, often neglected in
the past, and to provide them with alternate ways to gain
leadership experience as preparation for more complete
participation in their own labor organizations. While
women are entering the work force in increasing numbers,
and are staying in it, they have not moved into key leadership positions in labor unions in any great numbers.
Why not? What has held women back? We wanted to find out.

This study was designed to explore those questions.
Because the metropolitan office of Cornell's School of
Industrial and Labor Relations has had long and warm relationships with unions in New York City over the years,
we were easily able to find seven unions willing to work
intensively with us during the period of the study. Ad-
mittedly this was a self-selective process. Only unions
interested in education programs for their members and in
encouraging the further participation of their women members would come forward to work with us in an area so po-
tentially explosive. Why explosive? Because while most
of the seven unions have more than a 50 percent female
membership, the top leadership and staff posts in each are
held predominantly by men. Only an organization basically

vi

progressive and dedicated to the democratic involvement of
its members in the union would open its doors to investigation, devote the time of its leaders and staff to interviews, and make its membership available to questionnaire
survey, all in an effort to learn more about member attitudes toward the union itself.

To the extent that this self-selective process skews
the results of the study, it is a limitation. Yet those
who know labor unions will recognize that unions not so
dedicated would be reluctant to undertake such an investigation with its attendant risks. The seven unions that
were asked to join us in the study have been involved with
Cornell's labor extension work in the past, have a history
of experimenting with various kinds of education programs,
and were willing to consider new methods in an area of
growing concern and interest: the involvement of women
members in their unions. It has become popular to focus
attention on working women and on blue collar women in
particular; yet as recently as fall, 1972 when this study
began, this was not the case, and blue collar women were
all but forgotten. Other unions may now be as interested
as those seven were at an earlier date.

We have termed our project one of "action research,"
a term which may need a word of interpretation. By this
we mean research that is not only replicable but leads to
programs that utilize its findings. We are pleased to report that two studies, one in Michigan and one in New Zea-
land, are already using some of the instruments developed
in this study to test a quite different population of union
women. When the findings from these two studies are in,
we hope some comparative analyses will prove useful.

In terms of utilizing the findings of this study, an
ongoing program of labor studies and leadership training
for union women has been developed and launched in Cornell's metropolitan office, its first long-term session to
be oversubscribed. It has received the endorsement and
support of each of the unions that participated intensively
with us in the study. An interesting footnote is that the
racial composition of the union women in the program bears
out the study findings that minority women are especially
eager for education programs; two-thirds of the students
are minority women.

In presenting for public review the results of our
investigation into barriers to the participation of women
in labor unions, we have kept in the forefront our goal of
developing programs, especially with the seven unions
studied, to meet the needs of union women. If the programs

that emanate from the study are successful, they, too, may be replicated by trade unions and university labor extension programs. It is our hope that in areas outside New York City similar programs will become available to union women.

This report of the study is descriptive rather than analytical. We relate what we found as we found it, by and large letting the evidence speak for itself. The political reality is that only a few top posts in unions are held by women, and discrimination based on sex undoubtedly operates to some degree to bar women from leadership positions. We were searching, however, for additional reasons apart from gross bias that would explain the paucity of women in decision-making posts.

Clearly, any person who arrives at a position of top leadership in a union needs to be active in the union over a substantial period of time, and needs to spend a great deal of time pursuing this goal. To achieve it means, first of all, deciding that the goal is attainable; second, being willing to devote the time and energy needed to attain it; and third, actually _having_ the time to devote.

Women have special handicaps in fulfilling these requirements. Some are evident and our study findings confirm them. The dual careers of many women--family and work--interfere in obvious ways. A woman with children often interrupts her work career for months or years and consequently has difficulty reestablishing herself in the union. Furthermore, whether she stops work or not, she has traditional home responsibilities which are more time-consuming than those of men. Many women just do not have the time to be on call for union business during their early work years.

However, not all women are tied to the home. Many can make the time for other activities. Our concern was to learn what holds back those women, who do have time, from participating in their unions more actively, and to suggest ways that could help women to compensate for the years when heavy home responsibility limited their union activity more than it did that of the men.

The respondents in this study revealed there were handicaps other than the obvious ones which account for the low profile of women in union leadership:

- unexamined assumptions of men toward women's union roles
- the difficulty women have in envisioning themselves as leaders rather than helpers

- a deep-seated lack of confidence by women in their own abilities

These attitudes are made clear in Chapter 5, where we report in the words of men and women leaders themselves their views of the problems women have in attaining union leadership. For unless women can see various union leadership roles as attainable, they will not be willing to give the necessary time and effort to work toward achieving them. They tend to see themselves as less than adequate to handle the jobs in the union that they would like to hold. The women unionists seem to be seeking a heightened self-confidence and increased competency in practical leadership skills. Thus, when asked what would help them to take a more active role in the union, they answer "education." This speaks to three different points:

- The women (and men, too, but to a lesser degree) view their leaders as highly proficient, although not formally educated. The leaders are admired for their abilities in public speaking, dealing with management, and operating capably in a variety of situations. Women understand that these are essential skills and hope they can be acquired.
- Education is viewed by blue-collar workers as the magic that unlocks doors. To achieve it for their children they are willing to make extreme personal sacrifices. Their belief that it is the key for themselves to acquire the knowledge and skills needed for union leadership posts is no surprise.
- The response reveals that blue-collar women have a lack of trust in themselves and their own competence in participating on an equal basis with men in the union. Men with similar levels of formal education do not have to cope with this debilitating sense of inadequacy. The long years of acculturation to male dominance and the relatively recent acceptance of the equality of women's rights on the job doubtless are responsible. Thus women see education as a way of learning to express themselves, to gain vicariously some of the experiences and self-assurance that the men in the union have acquired during those years when women were less visible and more content to sit in the back of the bus.

We found women did not see themselves as top leaders, nor did they want to displace the top officers of their unions, whom they regard as doing a good job. Rather,

they want a bigger piece of the action, more chance to run
for local elected jobs, more respect from the male members
of the union when they speak at meetings, and more recognition for the union work they already do.

It is not the purpose of this report to back any union
against the wall and put it on the defensive. We believe
in labor unions as vehicles for social change, and today
they are moving, in many cases rapidly, toward change.
This is the first study of its kind, and it is only a beginning. We have suggested, in Chapter 6, other areas
where we feel further research would be useful, and that,
too, is only a start.

In designing the study described on the following
pages, we have had the invaluable advice of Dr. Lois Gray,
Assistant Dean of the New York State School of Industrial
and Labor Relations, Cornell University, and Director of
the metropolitan office, who has consistently been supportive of our work in developing programs for union women.
We have also called on John Drotning, ILR Dean of Education
and Public Service, for both suggestions and support, and
he, too, has been generous in his help. We are grateful
to Susan Berresford, Program Officer of the Ford Foundation, for her understanding help over the months of this
study and in formulation of the program of Trade Union
Women's Studies that succeeded the study and implemented
findings of our research. Robert Schrank, Project Specialist of the Ford Foundation, is another person for whose
knowledgeable advice we want to express our gratitude.
Without the support of the Ford Foundation the study would
not have been possible.

Most of all, however, we acknowledge here our debt
to the seven unions who worked with us in this study, and
to the New York City Central Labor Council, AFL-CIO, which
endorsed it. We are grateful to the leaders, staff, and
rank and file activists without whom the research would
not have been possible. Their cooperation at every step
of the way was unstinting. The work of the leaders and
members of these unions to achieve goals of union excel-
lence makes us proud to be part of the labor movement with
them. We were privileged to be able to share in their
work and learn more about it during the year of the study.
We have benefited from their ideas and experience in the
shaping of the present program of Trade Union Women's
Studies.

CONTENTS

LIST OF TABLES AND FIGURES

Trade Union Women

1

HERE TO STAY:
WOMEN IN THE WORK
FORCE AND LABOR UNIONS

Women have always worked to provide for their families. Where they once produced consumer goods at home, now woman work outside the home for the money with which to purchase them. Even as late as 1890 ours was a rural economy, with close to half the population living on farms. Farm women raised the food and livestock to feed their families, made their clothing and household articles, canned for the winter months, and sold any extra produce at market. The rapid urbanization of the American economy meant a total change in way of life but not in function: The need for women to contribute to the support of their families remained. Thus, women were drawn into factories and offices.

While the need for women to work has not changed, the outlook for women is vastly different today from what it was at the turn of the century. Then, a woman could expect to live an average of only 48 years and to lose half of her children before they grew to adulthood. She probably would not survive until the last of her children had grown, or, if she did, might well be widowed. Today her life span is 74 years. With the increased acceptance of birth control, she has far fewer children and can usually count on all her children living (of 526 born today, 500 will grow to adulthood). She can look forward to one-third of her life with her husband after her last child leaves home.

WOMEN IN THE WORK FORCE

The increasing number of women who work is an economic reality. Their work force participation rate outstrips predictions. The number of women in the labor

1

force was projected to increase by 5.6 million in the
1970s, but the estimate for 1975 was reached two years
earlier in 1973. Today 33 million women, 44.5 percent of
all adult females, now work outside the home. Original
estimates for 1973 projected 42.5 percent.

Figure 1.1 compares women in the population as a
whole with woman in the civilian labor force (1969).

At the rate women are presently employed, we can pre-
dict that 9 out of 10 women will work during some part of
their lives. This is in sharp contrast to the year 1900,
when only 2 out of 10 women over age 16 worked outside the
home. As recently as 1940, only 25 percent did.[1] The
average length of time married women can now expect to
spend in the work force is 25 years; single women will
average 45 years—the same as men. For the first time,
more than half the married women in the United States
worked at least part of the year. The trend is toward
women continuing to work after their children are born
(one-third now do so), and 36 percent of today's working
women have children under age six.[2] (See Table 1.1.)

Total employment leaped in the 1960s, with two-thirds
of the increase due to women. But myths die hard, and
there are still those who believe most of these women work
for pin money or to escape the boredom of suburban homes
filled with labor-saving gadgets. Not so. A total of 7.5
million working women is single, and over 6 million more
are divorced, widowed, or separated—the sole support of
their families. Another 4 million are married to men
earning less than $5,000.00 a year, who count on their
earnings to lift the family out of poverty.[3]

Women are found in each of some 500 occupational
categories, but cluster in only a few. (See Table 1.2.)

Rather than diversifying their occupations, women
increasingly swell the ranks of clerical and service workers. Over the last 30 years, the percent of clerical jobs
held by women rose from 50 to 74 percent, and their proportion of service jobs moved from 39 to 63 percent.

WOMEN'S EARNINGS

How does the earning power of women compare to that
of men? It is consistently lower. Rather than improving
their position as time goes on, full-time women workers
between 1955 and 1970 earned a shrinking percentage of
what men were paid; 1970 registered a modest upturn.

FIGURE 1.1

Characteristics of Women in the Population and in the Civilian Labor Force, 1969

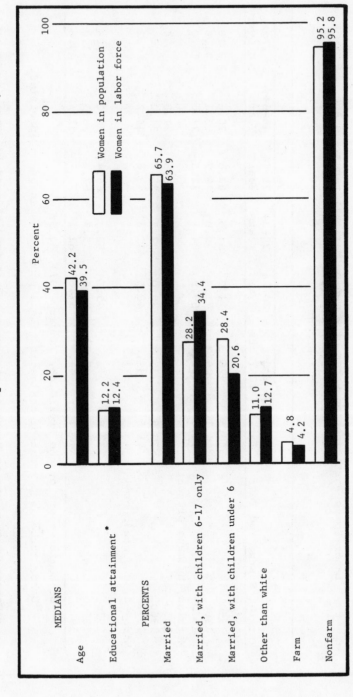

Source: U.S. Department of Labor, Bureau of Labor Statistics, "Women at Work", Monthly Labor Review 93, no. 6 (June 1970) : 21.
*Educational attainment describes women 18 years of age and over; all other characteristics apply to women 16 years of age and over.

TABLE 1.1

Labor Force Participation Rates of Women by Marital Status and Age,
1950, 1960, and 1972*
(percent)[a]

Marital Status and Year	Total	Age					
		Under 20 Years	20-24 Years	25-34 Years	35-44 Years	45-64 Years	65 Years and Over
Single							
1950	50.5	26.3	74.9	84.6	83.6	70.6	23.8
1960	44.1	25.3	73.4	79.9	79.7	75.1	21.6
1972	54.9	41.9	69.9	84.7	71.5	71.0	19.0
Married, husband present							
1950	23.8	24.0	28.5	23.8	28.5	21.8	6.4
1960	30.5	25.3	30.0	27.7	36.2	34.2	5.9
1972	41.5	39.0	48.5	41.3	48.6	44.2	7.3
Widowed, divorced, or separated							
1950	37.8	b	45.5	62.3	65.4	50.2	8.8
1960	40.0	37.3	54.6	55.5	67.4	58.3	11.0
1972	40.1	44.6	57.6	62.1	71.7	61.1	9.8

*Economic Report of the President, January 1973, p. 92.

[a]Labor force as percent of noninstitutional population in group specified.

[b]Not available.

Note: Data relate to March of each year. Data for 1950 and 1960 are for women 14 years of age and over; data for 1972 are for women 16 years of age and over.

Source: U.S. Department of Labor, Bureau of Labor Statistics.

TABLE 1.2

Women in Work Force, 1960-70

Major Job Categories	Percent of Jobs Held by Women 1960	Percent of Jobs Held by Women 1970	Total Jobs, Men and Women 1970	Change Since 1960 (+ and -)	Women's Share of Increase
All employed, 16 years and over	32.7	37.8	76,553,599	11,907,036	65.3
Professional, technical	38.1	40.1	11,351,138	4,127,897	43.7
Sales workers	35.7	39.3	5,445,374	801,590	60.1
Clerical workers	67.5	73.5	13,748,260	4,445,029	86.2
Craftsmen	2.9	4.9	10,609,630	1,856,162	14.5
Managers	14.4	19.9	6,371,149	963,259	28.6
Operatives	27.3	30.8	13,456,460	1,536,018	58.0
Service workers	52.3	62.8	8,627,356	3,171,650	61.0
Laborers	3.6	9.0	3,431,282	338,060	51.5
Farmers, farm workers	9.1	9.5	2,367,055	-1,580,845	--
Private household workers	96.5	96.8	1,109,858	-570,236	--
Select occupations					
Accountants	16.5	26.0	703,546	233,844	45.1
Dentists	2.1	3.4	90,801	3,914	33.0
Designers	18.1	23.6	108,788	43,115	31.9
Editors, reporters	36.5	40.4	146,925	46,644	48.7
Engineers	0.8	1.6	1,207,512	347,965	3.5
Funeral directors, embalmers	6.0	7.2	37,826	364	127.2
Lawyers, judges	3.4	4.8	272,401	63,705	9.5
Librarians	85.8	79.2	128,734	44,402	66.5
Nurses	97.6	97.3	829,691	248,402	96.6
Pharmacists	8.1	11.9	109,642	13,032	43.0
Physicians	6.7	9.0	280,929	51,258	20.3
Psychologists	30.5	38.2	27,830	16,136	43.8
Teachers, elementary and secondary schools	72.6	69.3	2,415,424	894,715	63.7
Real estate agents	23.5	31.9	262,161	64,232	57.7
Insurance agents	9.9	12.4	455,624	89,886	22.4
Bank tellers	69.0	86.2	249,243	121,616	104.2
Decorators, window dressers	45.7	57.5	69,960	17,796	91.7
Building superintendents	38.1	40.1	83,119	30,159	43.5
Bus drivers	9.8	27.8	235,942	52,902	72.7
Bartenders	11.0	20.9	188,769	16,893	121.4
Hair dressers, cosmetologists	88.0	90.1	471,536	165,678	92.6

Source: U.S. Census Bureau.

In 1955, women earned $63.90 for every $100 earned by men; in 1960, it fell to $60.80; and in 1968 to $58.20. (The 1890 ratio was 50 percent.) Women's 1970 earnings recovered some of the lost ground, $59.40 for every $100 earned by men, but did not rise to the ratio of 1960. (See Table 1.3.)

TABLE 1.3

Full-Time Workers, 1970 Median Wage or Salary

Race	Women	Men	Ratio Women to Men
Total	$5,403	$9,104	59.4
Minority	4,674	6,598	70.8
White	5,490	9,373	58.6

Source: U.S. Census Bureau.

That women workers are far more likely than men to hold low-skill, low-paying jobs is indicated by Table 1.4: 30.1 percent of all male workers in 1970 earned $7,000 a year or less, while 73.9 percent of all female workers did, and only 1.1 percent of all women workers earned $15,000 or more during that year.

TABLE 1.4

Earnings of Full-Time Year-Round Workers,
by Sex, 1970

Earnings	Women	Men
Number with earnings	15,476,000	36,132,000
Percent distribution	100.0	100.0
Less than $3,000	12.2	5.1
$3,000 to $4,999	32.5	8.8
$5,000 to $6,999	29.2	16.2
$7,000 to $9,999	19.3	30.1
$10,000 to $14,999	5.9	26.5
$15,000 and over	1.1	13.5

Source: U.S. Department of Commerce, Bureau of the Census, "Current Population Reports," no. 80, p. 60.

Not only do women earn less than most men, they also suffer from more unemployment. Figures for the first quarter of 1973 show white men 20 years old or over, with a 3.1 percent unemployment rate, white women with 4.5 percent unemployment, minority men with 5.5 percent unemployment, and minority women with a rate of 8.6 unemployment.[4] One-half of all the unemployed today are women, although they constitute 38.5 percent of the total work force.[5] The unemployment rate for married women with children is substantially higher than for those without (7.0 percent compared to 4.5 percent in the spring of 1971), evidence of the problem of matching the needs of children to the needs of industry. Women with preschool children show an unemployment rate in the same period of 10.2 percent.

Families headed by females constitute a disproportionate number of those living in poverty. While women head only one out of nine families in this country, 33 percent of these female-led families are poor. They constitute 43 percent of all poor families. This contrasts with 23 percent in 1959.[6] In almost 10 percent of these families, the women work full time.

WOMEN IN UNIONS

The disadvantage of women in the working place is compounded by the fact that relatively few are represented by labor unions. Literally millions of women are clustered in clerical and service jobs, areas traditionally hard to organize, or in factories throughout the rural areas of the United States, particularly in the South and Southwest. Only 13 out of every 100 women workers today are union members, some 4.8 million in all. The ratio of women unionists to women in the work force has actually dropped from 13.8 to 12.5 percent in the last 10 years.

Over half the women in unions belong to 12 labor organizations, although women constitute at least half of the membership in 26 trade unions.[7] (See Table 1.5.) American workers are not highly organized at best. Only 21.8 percent of all nonagricultural workers are organized in trade unions, down from 33.4 percent in 1956. Less than 10 percent of all white-collar workers and barely 11 percent of service workers are in unions, and only 17 percent of the country's 14.3 million government wage and salary workers are unionized.[8] (See Figure 1.2.) There are 212 labor and employee associations in this country, with 21.7 million members out of a work force of 89 million

TABLE 1.5

Women in the Labor Force
(approximate number of women members of labor unions,[a] 1970)

Union	Approximate Number of Women
American Federation of Labor and Congress of Industrial Organizations	
International Ladies' Garment Workers' Union	353,870
Amalgamated Clothing Workers of America	289,500
International Brotherhood of Electrical Workers	276,510
Retail Clerks International Association	b
Hotel and Restaurant Employees and Bartenders International Union	b
Communications Workers of America	231,860
International Union of Electrical, Radio, and Machine Workers	105,000
Building Service Employees' International Union	152,250
International Association of Machinists and Aerospace Workers	100,400
Textile Workers' Union of America	71,200
United Federation of Postal Clerks	37,260
Brotherhood of Railway, Airline and Steamship Clerks, Freight Handlers, Express and Station Employees	110,000
American Federation of Government Employees	b
Office and Professional Employees International Union	57,790
Amalgamated Meat Cutters and Butcher Workmen of North America	61,730
International Brotherhood of Bookbinders	31,240
Retail, Wholesale, and Department Store Union	70,000
American Federation of Teachers	88,290
United Rubber, Cork, Linoleum, and Plastic Workers of America	b
United Steelworkers of America	120,000
Bakery Workers	60,650
State, County Workers	146,680
Unaffiliated	
Alliance of Independent Telephone Unions	37,500
United Electrical, Radio, and Machine Workers of America	40,750
Federal Employees (NFFE)	50,000
International Union, United Automobile, Aerospace and Agricultural Implement Workers of America	193,130
International Union of District 50, United Mine Workers of America	25,200
International Brotherhood of Teamsters, Chauffeurs, Warehousemen, and Helpers of America	255,000

[a]Unions reporting 25,000 or more women members.

[b]Data not reported, but number of women believed to be significant.

Source: U.S. Department of Labor, Bureau of Labor Statistics, "Directory of National and International Labor Unions in the United States, 1972," Bulletin number 1750.

private and government wage and salary earners. The 1972
Biennial Survey of Labor Organizations of the Bureau of
Labor Statistics reported that, exclusive of professional
and state employee associations, 19.4 million workers belong to 177 national unions (excluding Canadian members of
these unions). A total of 113 of these unions is affiliated with the American Federation of Labor-Congress of Industrial Organizations (AFL-CIO).

FIGURE 1.2

Percent of Wage and Salary Workers in Labor Unions, 1970

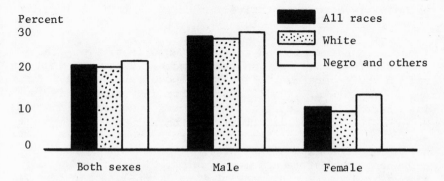

Although the proportion of the work force that is organized is falling, the actual number of union members is
rising. Both facts reflect the influx of women into jobs.
The AFL-CIO accounts for 16.5 million of the country's
union members, an increase of 529,000 between 1970 and
1972. Of this increase, 242,000 are women.
     Where do women stand in the national leadership and
staff positions in these unions? One in every five (20.7
percent) union members is a woman (up from 19.5 percent in
1968), but of the top leadership and staff positions reported in the 1971 Bureau of Labor Statistics Directory,
women hold only 70 posts in 47 of the 208 unions and employee associations. The American Guild of Variety Art-
ists, The American Nurses Association, The National Federation of Licensed Practical Nurses, and the Writers
Guild of America (Eastern section) report women presidents.[9] The following table shows the top elected and
appointed positions held by women as reported in the 1971
Directory by 114 AFL-CIO international and national unions.

Union Post	Number of Women
These posts most frequently are elective:	
President	1
Secretary-treasurer	2
Secretary	1
Treasurer	1
These posts tend to be appointive:	
Pension director	3
Organizing director	1
General counsel	1
Research director	4
Education director	2
Editor	2
Legislative representative	1
Public relations director	1

One department head in the AFL-CIO is a woman--the librarian; no women sit on the 39-member Executive Council of the federation, which is composed exclusively of union presidents. The 51 state labor federations (including Puerto Rico) report a total of six women staff members. No AFL-CIO regional directors are women. However, women are making their way onto an increasing number of international union Executive Boards, although not in numbers representative of female memberships. Labor's ranks have always included women, many of them front-line fighters in organizing drives and on picket lines. Some have made history, and some have died in the fight, unsung and unknown.

In the last decade or so, women--particularly minority women--have been moving into a number of national leadership posts which, if not yet the top reported positions, cannot be ignored. Nor can the thousands of women who hold local union offices and serve as shop stewards and on a host of trade union committees. There is a rising awareness in unions of their women members, and among women unionists, of themselves.

One signal of this direction is the increasing number of trade unions which, in convention assembled, are passing resolutions supporting equal pay and job advancement, child care legislation, and collective bargaining demands that improve maternity benefit and leave policies. They urge increased recruitment and fuller utilization of the talents of female staff members. More unions file equal-pay cases, insist on job posting, and divorce themselves from company policies that discriminate.

Are women unionists acting to further their own cause? There are signs of action. They have held state-wide education and legislative conferences. Some international unions with Women's Departments have begun to hold regional and national meetings for women members, publish newsletters, encourage the policing of equal-pay clauses in contracts, and insist on job posting.

The most significant occurrence, however, was the founding of the national Coalition of Labor Union Women (CLUW) in March 1974. Less than a year earlier, in June 1973, the idea was broached at the first Midwest Conference of Women Trade Union Leaders. At that time, more than 200 women from 20 states and 18 unions met to inaugurate plans for a nationwide conference of women in unions, to be held March 1974. That fall, women from the East Coast met in Philadelphia to consider a national organization, and meetings were held in the South and the West as well. In New York City, where an earlier group had been meeting and planning to bring union women together, over 500 women attended the First New York Trade Union Women's Conference one icy Saturday in January. It was just two months later that 3,200 women unionists spent three days "rapping and mapping," as Addie Wyatt, a leader from the Meat Cutters' Union, expressed it.

CLUW is only a fledgling organization at the time of this writing, but in the few months since it was founded it has inspired working women throughout the country. Local CLUW chapters, chartered under a structure that encourages broad representation of different unions, industries, and occupations, will work to implement in their own local unions the purposes of the national organization: to advance the position of women on the job, in the leadership of their unions, and through collective bargaining agreements and legislation to secure education and family benefits for working women.

IMPACT OF CHANGING SOCIAL ATTITUDES
ON TRADE UNION WOMEN

Social attitudes, while they have not caught up with the economic facts of women in the work force, are in the process of rapid change.

The drive to secure equality through legislation and legal action has affected many working women. It has meant new job opportunities, chances for upgrading, and the right to equal pay for equal work. The women's movement has had an impact on union women. In union conferences and programs we have heard women discuss this movement and find they are far more ready for action than they

11

are credited with being, particularly in the areas of
equal pay and child care. Most women, whether in or out
of the labor movement, are working for identical goals.
In fact, union women often acknowledge that those in the
women's movement have been "fighting our fight for us"
and indicate they would like now to prepare to do their
own fighting.

The rising education levels of both men and women
also make for changes: first, in contributing to the desire of more women to work (the higher the education level,
the higher the percentage of women in the work force) and
second, in changing the definitions of sex roles of both
men and women, particularly in the home. New views of home
responsibilities free women to participate in community and
union organizations on a more equal basis and lead to a
readier acceptance by men of this participation.

The women's movement is creating a new atmosphere for
union women as it alters attitudes in society generally.
Changes in the political involvement of women on national,
state, and local levels will mean new role models, new
self-awareness, new visibility, and new avenues for those
with leadership ability. Women are moving into more prom-
inent positions in appointed government posts, in business, and in church organizations. The media are changing
in their coverage of women and presumably will have a
strong influence on public opinion. It would be strange
indeed if change did not also come to trade union organizations.

For unions, the fact that more women remain in the
work force after they have children means far more than
an increased push for child care facilities. It means a
closing of the job and union experience gap that formerly
enabled men in their twenties and thirties to begin to
move up union and career ladders while women stayed at
home. By remaining in the work force, women will be able
to participate in both these areas. They will lose seniority less frequently--a loss that has meant starting
again at the bottom when they returned to work.

The most far-reaching effect of new union roles for
women, however, could be in the area of organizing unorganized women workers. Some 25 million women workers are
potential union members. Every union today with a majority of female members would, at the very least, double its
numbers if it were to organize its industry to the extent
that mass-production industries were organized. White-
collar, clerical, and sales workers, hospital and service
workers, farm and household workers and many more are

still not in unions. So far, labor leadership has not been able to do this job. Perhaps women reaching out to organize other women in this new and changing time can succeed.

WOMEN WORKERS IN NEW YORK

New York City is more highly organized than many other parts of the country, with one out of every three workers in trade unions.[10] Industrially it is a center of highly competitive labor-intensive firms producing largely consumer goods, firms small in size and offering fairly low wages. New York is also a city of offices, and by far the largest number of its women workers holds clerical jobs. Most of these workers are not yet in unions. Professional, technical, and related jobs engage the second largest number of women, with service jobs (not including private household) and factory operatives third and fourth.

What percentage of the total numbers in these industries is women? Private household workers are 95 percent female; almost three out of every four clerical workers are women, and more than two out of five service and factory workers. A total of 39 percent of the city's professional and technical workers is female, as are 35 percent of its sales force.[11] This latter group has a large potential for union organization.

Almost 2 million (1.85 million) women work in the city,[12] some 40 percent of all adult women (very close to the national average of 43 percent. This is 38.3 percent of all white women and 48.4 percent of women of minority races. Tables 1.6 and 1.7 are from the U.S. Department of Labor, Employment Standards Administration Women's Bureau, 1970. Table 1.6 shows what proportion of women are in various occupations, by ethnic group. Turning the figures around, Table 1.7 shows what proportion of the jobs held by women is held by Black and Puerto Rican women.

The international headquarters of some trade unions are in New York City, but most are not. The affiliated local unions in New York are often large and function with a great deal of independence.[13] One of the most powerful forces on the city labor scene is the Central Labor Council of the AFL-CIO, headed by Harry Van Arsdale, Jr. Most New York City AFL-CIO unions are affiliated with it. One woman sits on its Executive Board.

13

TABLE 1.6

Labor Force and Occupational Status of New York
City Women, by Ethnic Group, 1970
(women 16 years of age and over)

Labor Force Status and Occupation	All Women	Black	Puerto Rican Origin
Labor force			
Number	2,878,027	370,873	80,940
Participation rate	41.3	47.3	28.8
Women as percent of all workers	38.8	46.2[a]	32.4[b]
Occupation of employed			
Number	2,745,814	351,486	74,640
Percent	100.0	100.0	100.0
Professional, technical, kindred workers	17.0	12.0	6.6
Managers, administrators (except farm)	3.5	1.8	1.7
Sales workers	6.8	2.8	4.2
Clerical workers	40.9	34.2	33.7
Craftsmen, foremen	1.5	1.5	2.4
Operatives (including transport)	12.9	14.0	37.3
Nonfarm laborers	0.6	0.8	1.0
Farm workers	0.3	0.3	0.1
Service workers (except private household)	13.6	21.7	12.1
Private household workers	2.8	11.0	0.8
Last occupation of experienced unemployed			
Worked during last 10 years	113,589	16,196	5,070
Percent	100.0	100.0	100.0
Professional, technical, managerial workers	10.9	6.3	3.4
Sales workers	7.2	4.4	4.0
Clerical workers	29.6	26.5	17.5
Operatives (including transport)	32.2	30.9	59.3
Other blue-collar workers	3.3	3.9	6.0
Farm workers	0.4	0.3	0.7
Service workers (except private household)	13.8	18.0	8.0
Private household workers	2.7	9.6	1.1

[a]Black women workers as percent of black work force.

[b]Puerto Rican-origin women workers as percent of Puerto Rican-origin work force.

Source: U.S. Department of Commerce, Bureau of the Census, "Census of Population: 1970. General Social and Economic Characteristics, PC(1)-C34."

TABLE 1.7

Minority Women Workers in New York City as Proportion
of All Women Workers, by Occupation, 1970
(women 16 years of age and over)

| | | As Percent of All Women Workers | |
Occupation	All Women Workers	Black	Puerto Rican Origin
Occupation of employed			
Total	2,745,814	12.8	2.7
Professional, technical, kindred workers	465,760	9.0	1.1
Managers, administrators (except farm)	97,142	6.3	1.3
Sales workers	187,512	5.3	1.7
Clerical workers	1,122,767	10.7	2.2
Craftsmen, foremen	41,752	12.4	4.3
Operatives (including transport)	354,300	13.9	7.8
Nonfarm laborers	16,688	17.2	4.6
Farm workers	8,315	11.1	0.9
Service workers (except private household)	373,774	20.4	2.4
Private household workers	77,804	49.6	0.8
Last occupation of experienced unemployed			
Worked during last 10 years	113,589	14.3	4.5
Professional, technical, managerial workers	12,340	8.3	1.4
Sales workers	8,123	8.9	2.5
Clerical workers	33,580	12.8	2.6
Operatives (including transport)	36,606	13.7	8.2
Other blue-collar workers	3,761	16.9	8.1
Farm workers	403	10.4	9.4
Service workers (except private household)	15,680	18.6	2.6
Private household workers	3,096	50.2	1.8

Source: U.S. Department of Commerce, Bureau of the
Census, "Census of Population: 1970. General Social and
Economic Characteristics, PC(1)-C34."

In inviting seven local unions to join us in this
year-long study, we selected one white-collar and six
blue-collar unions in representative New York industries:
manufacturing, service, government, and retail. Each
union has its own personality. We hope the reader will
enjoy getting to know all seven through these pages.
The following chapters will

- present the major hypotheses of the study and indicate the role of women members in the New York
  City local unions surveyed as a preliminary to
  the study (Chapter 2);
- briefly describe the seven unions that cooperated
  in the study of rank and file members and introduce by means of related study findings the men
  and women who belong to them (Chapter 3);
- describe the union activity of the men and women
  of these seven unions and what changes are needed
  to increase it (Chapter 4);
- develop profiles of union women: how they see
  themselves, how union leaders see them, and how
  they are viewed by male co-workers (Chapter 5);
- discuss the implications of the study for union
  women and their unions and what these suggest in
  the way of new directions for the unions surveyed.
  A description is included of a pilot program in
  Trade Union Women's Studies which was undertaken
  as a result of the findings of this study (Chapter 6).

NOTES

1. Ruth Jordan, "Women's Share of Economic Pie
Shrinking," The Butcher-Workman (April 1973): 8.
2. U.S. Department of Labor, Employment Standards
Administration, Women's Bureau, "Day Care Facts," Pamph-
let 16 (rev.), 1973.
3. U.S. Department of Labor, Employment Standards
Administration, Women's Bureau, "Why Women Work," June
1973 (revised).
4. U.S. Department of Labor, Bureau of Labor Statistics, Government Printing Office, Employment and Earnings 20, no. 1 (July 1973): 53, Table A43.
5. U.S. Department of Labor, Monthly Labor Review 93,
no. 6 (June 1970): 14.
6. The New York Times, July 5, 1973, p. 25.

7. U.S. Department of Labor, Women's Bureau, <u>Handbook on Women Workers, 1969</u>, p. 83.

8. U.S. Department of Labor, Bureau of Labor Statistics, "Selected Earnings and Demographic Characteristics of Union Members, 1970," Report 417, 1972, p. 2.

9. Since publication of the <u>Directory</u>, a woman has been elected president of the 1,100,155-member National Education Association and of the Washington State Employees Association (Supplement no. 1 to the <u>Directory</u>).

10. Alice H. Cook and Lois S. Gray, "Labor Relations in New York City," <u>Industrial Relations</u> 5, no. 3 (May 1966): 86, 87.

11. U.S. Department of Labor, Employment Standards Administration, Women's Bureau, "Women Workers in New York, 1970," December 1972.

12. U.S. Department of Labor, Employment Standards Administration, "Women Workers in Regional Areas and in Large States and Metropolitan Areas, 1971," Table 2, p. 5.

13. Cook and Gray, op. cit., p. 91.

The rapid rise in union membership among working women
has coincided with major changes in labor law and practice
relating to sex discrimination. There is no doubt that
unions are increasingly interested in and concerned about
their women members. As female membership rises and wom-
en's needs receive new attention, union leaders seek and
expect higher involvement from their women members.

What keeps women from participating more fully in
union affairs? Speculation has centered on such factors as
tradition, the additional burdens a working wife and mother
carries, and the lack of time or opportunity for training
and experience during those years when men are active in
their union and women busy with young children. But these
answers were only speculative, and it seemed time to study
the question in depth.

This study, then, was designed to learn more about
how women see themselves in relation to their unions, and
how union officers and men in the unions view the low involvement of women on decision-making levels.

First, the local unions in New York City having a
substantial number or a majority of women members were
surveyed. Next, we focused on seven of these locals, each
affiliated with a national or international union having
members in the United States and sometimes Canada:

> Amalgamated Meat Cutters and Retail Food Store
>   Employees' Union, Local 342
> New York Metro Area Postal Union (formerly the
>   Manhattan-Bronx Postal Union)
> International Ladies' Garment Workers' Union,
>   Local 22

American Federation of State, County, and
   Municipal Employees, District Council 37,
   Custodial Assistants, Local 1597
International Union of Electrical Workers,
   Local 463
United Store Workers' Union
Drug and Hospital Employees' Union, District 1199

While we shall describe for the reader the way in
which each of the locals of our study fits into the structure of its parent union, essentially every local works
quite independently, handling its own grievances with management and solving its local problems with the industry.
A microcosm of the international, the local union is a more
manageable unit and lends itself to closer study. Figure
2.1 depicts the relationship between a local and its international.

IDENTIFYING THE PROBLEM

The barriers to the participation of women in unions
were divided into the following groups for examination:

1. Cultural-societal-personal: This group includes
a number of diverse but related barriers: husband's attitudes toward wife's participation; transportation problems;
inadequate child care and baby-sitting; fear of going out
at night; lack of time because of home and child care
duties; low self-esteem; feelings a woman often has that
her participation does not matter, that "men can do it better," and other indications of an acceptance of a stereo-
typed societal role; involvement in community or church
organizations that affect her time for union commitment;
level of education; income.
2. Job-related: Here we find barriers include the
experience gap of the woman returning to the job market,
dead-end jobs at entry levels, fear of competing with male
workers, fear of supervisors if a woman worker becomes
"aggressive," lack of upgrading and training opportunities,
and separate job lines for men and women.
3. Union-related: There may be union-related barriers to her participation, such as little encouragement
to run for office, no offices open, being relegated to role
of "secretary" if she serves on committees, collective bargaining demands of special interest to women discouraged,
little opportunity to train for active union role, and
few role models.

FIGURE 2.1

Structure of a Typical International Trade Union and its Local Union Affiliates.

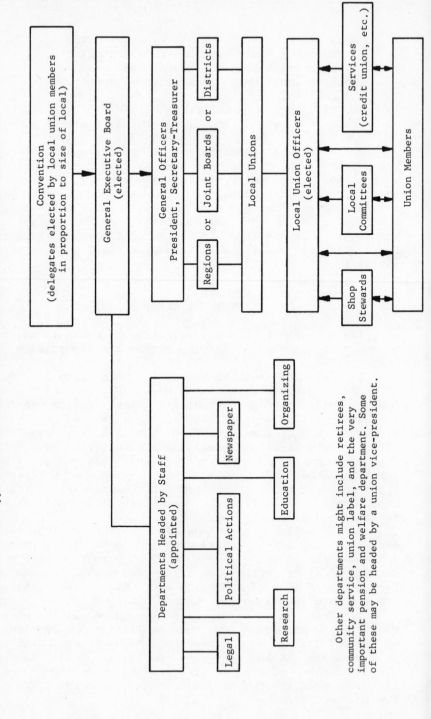

Other departments might include retirees, community service, union label, and the very important pension and welfare department. Some of these may be headed by a union vice-president.

INITIAL PHASE--OVERVIEW SURVEY
OF NEW YORK CITY LOCALS

The aim of the first part of the study was to achieve
an overview of the participation level of women members of
New York City local unions that have jurisdiction in industries with approximately one-third or more women workers. It was designed to answer the following questions:

1. What percentage of the local's members is women?
What kinds of jobs do they hold? Are there opportunities
for advancement?
2. How many leadership positions (from steward up to
president) do women hold in the local? How successful are
women felt to be in these positions? What proportion of
women members attends union meetings? Participates in
committees?
3. What is the attitude of the union's leadership
toward the barriers to women's job and union advancement?
Are some of these regarded as surmountable? Is there an
education or upgrading program which the union sponsors or
with which it cooperates?

Of the 195 local unions that were identified as having
substantial female memberships, questionnaires were returned by 92 unions on behalf of 108 locals (55.5 percent
response). These unions represent a total membership of
541,336 and a female membership of 284,189.
The summary of local union leadership opinions presented in this chapter is not a systematic review of critical issues. However, it highlights some fundamental assumptions and attitudes of the unions most concerned with
women's participation: those having many women members
and leaders considering it important to return the questionnaire. The opinions provide some measure of the extent of women's involvement at various leadership levels.
Coupled with the information on actual union positions
held by women, they provide invaluable clues in our search
for the reasons for the low self-image of women, revealed
in later chapters as the study unfolds.
The unions that responded to the overview questionnaire differ in size and percent of women members. All
returns from unions with less than 10 percent female membership were discarded; the remainder was grouped by the
proportion of their membership that was female. In this
way, the skills, advancement opportunities, and union participation of women in unions with large numbers of women
can be compared to those of unions with smaller numbers.

21

The responding unions tended to be of medium size, ranging between 1 and 10,000 members, and to represent manufacturing, clerical, or other service occupations. The women members are likely to work at semi-skilled jobs and to have relatively few job-advancement opportunities.

BACKGROUND OF SURVEY UNIONS: INDUSTRY, SIZE, WOMEN'S JOBS

The largest number of unions that returned overview questionnaires represents workers in manufacturing (45 percent), particularly the garment industry (25 percent). Next are those unions organized in a variety of service and clerical occupations (43 percent). Unions of professional employees account for 12 percent of the respondents. This response differs from the 1970 labor force distribution for women in New York State as a whole in two signal ways: Manufacturing is overrepresented and clerical workers are underrepresented. These differences are attributable in part to the concentration of the garment industry in New York City and in part to the way the labor force is organized into unions. The first circumstance increases the number of manufacturing occupations represented in the response, and the second, since many clerical workers are not members of unions, decreases their number in the response. Professional, technical, and kindred occupations account for 17 percent of female employees in the state and are somewhat underrepresented in the overview, attributable to the lag in unionization of this group.

Most of the responding unions have between 1,000 and 10,000 members; 16 percent were larger than 10,000; over a quarter were below 1,000. This spread is characteristic of New York City generally, where local unions are typically about 7,500, but where very large unions of 30,000 and more exist side by side with small organizations of a few hundred. (See Table 2.1.)

Although the greatest interest lies in the answers of unions with at least a quarter of their membership composed of women, the answers of those with fewer numbers are included for comparison purposes. As the participation level of women in the responding unions is described hereafter, it will be presented in terms of the proportion of women members. Table 2.2 sets forth these proportions.

The level of the jobs held by women in responding unions shows a definite bias toward skilled manufacturing as represented by sewing-machine operators. In every

case, the level reported is a judgment by the union leadership of the job skill of most, but not all, of their women
members. The largest number of women performs semiskilled
work.

TABLE 2.1

Size of Responding Unions

Size of Union	Number of Unions	Percentage of Total
Below 1,000	24	26.1
1,000-9,999	53	57.6
10,000-20,000	9	9.8
More than 20,000	6	6.5
Total	92	100.0

TABLE 2.2

Female Membership of Responding Unions

Percentage of Female Members	Number of Unions	Percentage of Total
10-25	17	18.5
25-50	27	29.4
More than 50	48	52.1
Total	92	100.0

Where the responding union was predominantly female,
its members tended to hold semiskilled jobs in occupations
often thought of as typically women's, for example, in retail, clerical, or hospital work. On the other hand,
unions indicating they had less than a majority of women
members reported that women members tended to hold unskilled jobs. This reflects the vertical nature of manufacturing industries other than garment, where large numbers of women still are found at this level. (See Table
2.3.)

Two-thirds of the jobs women hold provide few advancement opportunities or, more often, none at all. Those
unions with very high female memberships are significantly
more likely than others to offer only entry-level jobs, a
fact which leads to the suspicion that women have been
relegated to these jobs. (See Table 2.4.)

23

TABLE 2.3

Skill Level of the Jobs Held by Women in Survey Unions

Skill Level	Number of Unions	Percentage of Total
Unskilled	16	18.6
Semiskilled	37	43.0
Skilled	29	33.7
Combination	4	4.7
Total respondents	86	100.0

TABLE 2.4

Advancement Opportunities of Women Grouped by the
Proportion of Women Members in Those Unions

Advancement Opportunity	All Unions	Unions with 10 to 25 Percent Female Membership	Unions with 25 to 50 Percent Female Membership	Unions with More than 50 Percent Female Membership
Most jobs stop at entry level	34.2%	30.8%	25.0%	40.5%
At least one opportunity for advancement	31.7	46.2	33.3	26.2
Numerous opportunities	25.3	15.4	33.3	23.8
Not relevant	5.1	7.6	0.0	7.1
Combinations	3.7	0.0	8.4	2.4
Total unions	100.0	100.0	100.0	100.0

A large number of the survey unions report that there
is a union- or company-sponsored upgrading program available. Of the 28 locals reporting such a program, half represent either municipal employees or telephone workers.
Eight belong to District Council 37 of the American Federation of State, County, and Municipal Employees, which has
most of the city agencies organized. This giant union has
intensive education and upgrading programs, which will be
described in more detail in Chapter 3. Six locals are organized in the telephone industry, where company-sponsored
training programs long have been available.

Of the remaining 15 locals, 5 are in service occupations often identified as female: retail store, hotel, cleaners, hospital, janitorial. Programs of some locals in this group are available only in certain shops. The unions in this group represent about 73,000 women, 45,000 of whom belong to District 1199 Drug and Hospital Employees' Union (1972 figures). This union has pioneered in upgrading for paraprofessionals, and its vigorous program is also described in a later chapter. Six locals represent manufacturing occupations and account for the fewest women to whom upgrading training is available. As with other unions, the training may not be offered to all shops. Three locals represent combinations of professional, clerical, and paraprofessional women. The largest of these is the United Federation of Teachers (UFT) with an estimated female membership of 49,000. The UFT reports in-service training for teachers and also a college program for paraprofessionals that is subsidized by the union.

PARTICIPATION OF WOMEN IN UNION AFFAIRS

With this background description of the unions in the overview survey and of the jobs of their women members, we need to add the caution stated at the outset, that the unions that returned questionnaires can be assumed to be those most likely to have an interest in women's participation. The 44 percent that did not respond cannot be judged on the basis of these returns.

Union leaders in the overview survey were asked, "Do you think women generally take as much interest in the union as men?" By far the largest number of unions (61 percent) replied yes; 4 percent were "not sure"; the remainder thought women were less interested than men. On the other hand, asked whether they considered the willingness of women to run for election to be high or low, most responding leaders thought it to be low (62 percent) although more than a third thought it high. Women are seen by union leaders as less willing to run for election than to participate in committees or attend membership meetings. But their willingness to run is higher than their representation in union staff positions, over which they have little control. (See Table 2.5.)

The degree of their involvement in committee work confirms the general opinion of leaders that the interest of women is high. Committee work is a key indicator of interest since it requires effort as well as time; attendance at membership meetings is another indicator since it requires, at the minimum, a commitment of time. Yet despite this interest, women do not appear to have the confidence to risk running for election. This is the first of the cumulative evidence that the societal view of women as helpers, instead of leaders, is one that women themselves share.

TABLE 2.5

Union Leaders' Judgment of the Level
of Women's Participation
(in percent)

	High	Low
Women's participation on committees	61.6	38.4
Women's attendance at membership meetings	42.0	58.0
Women's willingness to run for election	37.7	62.3
Number of women in union staff positions	31.8	68.2

The union responses have particular significance when they are separated and grouped by the proportion of women members represented. The evidence is that where women constitute a large proportion of union membership, their participation is judged to be higher than where they are heavily outnumbered. But over and above that evidence is a dramatic difference in their willingness to lead; 72 percent of the unions that registered a high willingness among their women to run for election were unions with a majority of women members. (See Table 2.6.)

The conclusion appears inescapable that women are more able to view themselves as potential leaders where they are least likely to face male competition.

Looked at another way, however, the data reveal that men are judged dominant in all indexes of participation with one exception, committee work in unions where there are a majority of women members.

So far we have discussed the perception of the responding union leaders as to the level of interest and participation of women in their locals. Now let us examine the facts as measured by the number of women who actually hold top posts and other supportive positions.

A total of 18 of the 92 responding unions has a woman president; this is the post held least frequently by a

woman. As would be expected, most unions with a woman
president have a majority of women members. One factor to
be considered is that the presidency of local unions is
often an unpaid or at best a partially salaried position
in the smaller locals.

TABLE 2.6

Union Leaders' Judgment of Women's Participation,
Grouped by the Proportion of Women Members
in Their unions

	Unions with 10 to 25 Percent Female Membership	Unions with 25 to 50 Percent Female Membership	Unions with More than 50 Percent Female Membership
High participation in committees	11.8	40.8	66.7
High attendance at membership meetings	11.8	33.3	47.9
High willingness to run for election	11.8	22.2	43.8
High number of women in staff positions	0.0	25.9	31.3

The top position most frequently held by women is as
a member of the local's Executive Board. This is an un-
salaried union post held by rank and file members who
work full time in plant, shops, or offices. Its purpose
is to link union officers and staff more directly to the
shop membership. The Executive Board is a legislative
body with authority to approve or propose policy, which
the officers and staff then carry out. However, it may,
to varying degrees, receive instructions on how to take
policy decisions to the membership, hear announcements of
what union events are planned, and recruit membership
support for both. The board also serves as a source of
feedback on policies; its members are expected to keep the
leadership informed on rank and file attitudes toward
proposals or actions. Its members are usually shop stewards and committee chairmen and are elected to the position by general ballot of the entire local. This is a
post of honor, and the abler activists usually will be

chosen for it. Where women are found in a union-wide position, this tends to be the one. A total of 75 percent of the unions surveyed does have women represented on their Executive Boards, yet 10 percent of the unions with a majority of women members do not.

The next top post most frequently held by women is that of secretary (recording or corresponding) or sometimes secretary-treasurer. It is an unpaid position except in large locals. The holder of the office is a full member of the executive committee, voting and attending all meetings, but usually the job requires more concentration on the recording of decisions than on making them. Where the function is combined with that of the treasurer, it is generally understood to require good record-keeping skills and to be a responsible post, though often removed from budgeting and planning functions. About 45 percent of the unions in the survey have women secretaries, treasurers, or secretary-treasurers.

The most important cog in local union administration is the business agent, also called "union representative," and sometimes "organizer." It is the business agent's job to adjust grievances not solved by the shop steward and to see that union working rules and contract provisions are observed. The agent fills many other roles as needed: counselor to individual members, price negotiator for piecework, organizer of unorganized shops, strike leader, and adviser on new contract demands. The business agents usually devote full time to their union duties and are paid by the union. Not all locals have their own agents; small ones are often served by the agents of the union's joint board or council of their industry (see Figure 2.1). Of the unions surveyed, 30 percent had a woman business agent; almost all of them (82 percent) were employed by unions with a majority of women members. While this is not surprising, it is worth noting that 52 percent of the unions with a majority of women had no union representative who was female.

Women fare somewhat better as directors of Welfare and Pension Funds, Credit Unions, or in other staff jobs such as newspaper editor and education director; 36 percent of the unions report a woman at that level. Unions with less than a majority of women members were more likely to employ women as staff directors than as business agents; for unions with a majority of women members, the number having a woman in either a chief staff position or as business agent was the same (48 percent in both cases). Table 2.7 sets forth the number of unions that have at least one woman in each of the union-wide positions.

28

TABLE 2.7

Unions with Women in Union-Wide Position

Position	Number of Unions	Percent of Total
President	18	19.6
Vice-president	26	28.3
Secretary, treasurer, secretary-treasurer	41	44.6
Other executive board member, trustee	69	75.0
Business agent, organizer, union representative	28	30.4
Chief staff (Welfare, Pension Fund, and so on)	33	35.9

In order to see whether the women in these union-wide positions were more than isolated cases, the number of women in the positions was compared to the total number of positions available. Some general statements can be made on the basis of the data.

Women clearly do not hold positions representative of their numbers in most of the responding unions. Although 52 percent of the unions surveyed have a majority of women members, only a third have a majority of women in union-wide posts; 13 percent have no women at all in any top post. When the responses are related to the proportion of women members (Table 2.8), we find:

1. Unions with a majority of women members are far more likely than others to approximate the same proportions in their top positions; about half of them do.

2. Unions with a large proportion but not a majority of women members are somewhat less likely to reach the same proportions in their union-wide positions.

3. Unions with the lowest proportion of women members (10 to 25 percent) are by far the least likely to reach the same proportions in their union-wide positions.

More specifically, only two local unions with a majority of women members report that no women hold any of the top positions, while 41 percent of the unions with the lowest female membership (10 to 25 percent) have no women in these key posts.

TABLE 2.8

Number of Women in Union-Wide Posts as a Percentage
of Total Posts Available

Percentage of the Total Posts That Are Held by Women	All Unions	Unions with 10 to 25 Percent Female Membership	Unions with 25 to 50 Percent Female Membership	Unions with More than 50 Percent Female Membership
No woman in any post	13.0	41.2	11.1	4.2
Below 10 percent of the posts	4.3	5.9	11.1	0.0
10 to 25 percent of the posts	13.0	17.6	22.2	6.3
25 to 50 percent of the posts	27.2	0.0	29.6	37.5
More than 50 percent of the posts	32.6	5.9	11.1	52.1
No answer	10.9	29.4	14.8	2.1

In Table 2.8 the number of women in union-wide posts is presented as a percentage of the total positions available. The 92 responding unions are further broken down by their proportions of women members. The positions described are president, vice-president, secretary-treasurer, other executive board members and trustees, business agent, organizer, union representative, chief staff director (Welfare, Pension Fund, and so on).

The factual data appear to bear out the opinions of union leaders that women have high interest in the union where there are many of them, and that where there are fewer, their interest is reported at declining levels corresponding to their proportions in the union. We identify this process with three elements. The first is that where there are successful women activists to inspire rank and file members as models, women's participation rises; they see a future for themselves in union activity. The second is that male leaders are more willing to make room for

women as their number increases. And the third, reinforc-
ing an earlier observation, is that women appear to be
more able to view themselves as potential leaders, rather
than just helpers, where they are least likely to face
male competition.

What about lower-level leadership positions? Are
women more likely to be there? The evidence is that they
are. Women hold a considerably higher proportion of rank
and file leadership posts than key positions. For example, almost three-quarters of the responding unions with
a majority of women members also have a majority of women
in these rank and file posts, while about half report a
majority in their union-wide posts.

The rank and file positions that unions are most
likely to report at least one woman holding are shop steward (66 percent of the unions), chief shop steward (49
percent), or committee member (39 percent) where committees are present. Only one union of those that answered
the question has no female steward or committee member.
All responding unions have a woman in some rank and file
position. Chairmen of committees are least likely to be
female; 32 percent of the unions report having at least
one woman as chairman of a committee. The comparison of
rank and file posts with more important leadership positions is complicated by the fact that many unions do not
have a full complement of the posts for which they were
asked to give data; others simply did not fill in the information. Unions with the fewest women members were
least likely to answer the question, while those with a
majority of women members appeared most ready to answer,
and indeed their women are well represented in rank and
file leadership positions. Table 2.9 presents the data
and relates it to the proportions of women members. The
four rank and file positions described are chief shop
steward or chief delegate, shop steward and delegate
grievance committee member, chairman of a committee, and
committee member.

In all responding unions, women appear to be interested in union affairs and willing to offer their time and
service, but they are far more likely to make their contribution from a relatively low union position. These
findings, together with the comments of union leaders related below, suggest that women might participate more if
their activity were encouraged, and they might be available for higher position if higher positions were open.

As noted earlier, most of the responding unj   leaders consider women members to be as interested ın the

union as men, although men are judged dominant in all indexes of participation except that of committee member in
unions with a majority of women members. When those who
consider women's participation to be high are asked why,
the reason most often given is that there are many women
in those unions and, consequently, they are interested in
union activities and responsibilities.

TABLE 2.9

Number of Women in Rank and File Posts as
a Percentage of Total Posts Available

Percentage of the Total Posts That Are Held by Women	All Unions	Unions with 10 to 25 Percent Female Membership	Unions with 25 to 50 Percent Female Membership	Unions with More than 50 Percent Female Membership
No woman in any post	0.0	0.0	0.0	0.0
Below 10 per-cent of the posts	3.3	17.6	0.0	0.0
10 to 25 per-cent of the posts	11.9	23.5	14.8	6.3
25 to 50 per-cent of the posts	22.8	11.8	51.9	10.4
More than 50 percent of the posts	42.4	11.8	11.1	70.8
No answer	19.6	35.3	22.2	12.5

When those who consider women's participation to be
low are asked why, the three most common answers are

1. fear of the streets and subways in the late
   evening hours,
2. family responsibility,
3. lack of interest--"same as the men."

The overview questionnaire probed the reasons for the
level of women's participation in four specific areas:

attendance at membership meetings, activity on committees, willingness to run for election, and proportions in staff positions. The following explanations were given for high attendance of women at membership meetings (in addition to the one cited above—large numbers of women members):

- They come to check up on leadership.
- They are concerned about all matters that affect them and are prepared to give them their personal attention.
- Interest is strong, particularly at contract time.
- Women usually side with the conservative or non-militant group. They are more interested in benefits.
- They are very enthusiastic; it is easier to get women to participate than men.
- They are more active, more dedicated, and more willing to take the time.

What do leaders have to say about women's participation in committees? Both apathy and interest are cited. Participation is said to be high because:

- They are smarter than men.
- Women dominate because of low wages and they want to better themselves.
- The work can be done during the day, and so they will not be traveling home after dark.
- Union activity draws older women with grown families who have the time to participate and see the opportunity to better themselves and their co-workers by becoming involved (single women too).

Other comments:

- Those women who accept responsibility generally perform at a higher level.
- Would like women on committees because they are usually more practical and tend less toward theatrics.
- If the results of the subject are important to them, usually some of the women will participate. As with men, more than not seem not interested.

What makes women willing to run for election? A good chance of winning is the most frequent answer. Why are women unwilling to run (and 62 percent of the leaders say they are)? Curiously enough, no leader mentions a good chance of losing as the explanation. Reasons that are mentioned include:

- They have a tendency to feel that they are not leaders, and many of them expect from past history to see a male in charge.
- Fear that positions might be too demanding, above their heads. Reluctant to take responsibility and fail.
- Misguided sense of inferiority.
- No encouragement.
- I am amazed at the lack of ambition; women are apathetic.
- They are scared.

Finally, when leaders of the few unions that have a high proportion of women staff positions were asked why, the reason of each was that there simply are a large number of women members. Where the proportion of female staff members is low, these reasons were given:

- Resignations and retirements are infrequent. The union is not expanding so we do not need new staff.
- Language barriers make them hesitant.
- It is hard to deal with our membership.

CONCLUSIONS

The results of the overview survey indicate that some avenues are available to unions that wish to increase the interest and involvement of their women members.

One that is not new but has not been widely applied to women is to expand the opportunities for advancement on the job. A total of 66 percent of the responding unions reports little or no chance for their women to move ahead from the jobs they now hold. A further measure that would tie the interests of women to the unions would be the presence of training programs so that women could prepare themselves to qualify for better jobs as the jobs become available.

Confronted with the conflicting evidence of interest in the union and unwillingness to take leadership responsibility, unions may find ways to solve the problem in the suggestions of the women themselves as reported in the second phase of the study. At this time, however, we conclude from evidence of the overview survey that women tend to contribute to the union as helpers to men who are in more responsible positions. They belong to committees in large numbers, but 68 percent of the committee chairmen are men. Almost three-quarters of the unions with a

majority of women members have a majority of women in rank
and file positions, but only about half of them have a
majority in union-wide positions. No union is unrepre-
sented by women in rank and file posts, but 13 percent
have no woman in any positions at the top.

The evidence also indicates that where women are a
sizable proportion of the membership, their general participation is higher and they appear far more willing to
run for election. Leaders in those unions comment glow-
ingly on the value and level of participation of the women
members. Why do women behave differently in unions where
they are fewer in number? Where unions have many women
members, is it clear to the women that their assistance is
needed and will be important? Does this lead to high involvement? Do those who become active as a result serve
as role models for their union sisters?

The data of the first phase of the study raise questions that can only be answered by a closer inspection of
particular unions and the views of the women themselves.

1. How widespread is the fear of the streets and subways at night? Does this markedly affect women's participation in union events? Have other meeting times been
tried and were they successful?

2. To what extent does a woman's family responsibilities restrict her union activity? Do certain ages or
numbers of children limit her more than others? Do husbands affect the union activity of their wives?

3. Do women tend to be apathetic toward their unions?
Why are they thought to be indifferent in some unions but
not others? What methods are used to encourage membership
participation? Do these work equally well for men and
women?

4. Do women feel that men should run the union? Are
they afraid of responsibility? Of failing?

5. What do women think the union could do to make it
easier for them to become active unionists?

SECOND PHASE OF THE STUDY

The men and women members of seven local unions were
questioned about their participation and what barriers
they consider stand in the way of greater activity. Although the responses from members in the different unions
often coincide, it is necessary to review the experiences
and attitudes of the members within the context of their
own unions. This we begin to do in Chapter 3.

35

3

Seven local unions in the New York City area were in-
vited to proceed with us to an in-depth study of the participation of their members in the union. The locals were
selected to represent a cross section of organized workers
in private industry and public employment in the city and
to represent a membership at least 25 percent female.
Among the unions chosen, female membership ranged from 25
to 90 percent.

All seven unions accepted the invitation and cooperated fully in the study. They wanted to know more about
why their members did or did not participate at various
levels of union activity and to discover what the barriers
might be to their further participation. One union described the reasons in its newspaper for its cooperation
in the study:

> ## 342 Joins Cornell in Study of Union Women
>
> What stands in their way? . . . What can
> the union do to tackle some of these prob-
> lems, as in the past it has won victories
> in higher wages, shorter hours, and better
> working conditions for all its members?
> . . . Through working with Cornell on
> this study, we will learn more about the
> day-to-day problems our women members
> face, and perhaps come up with some new
> programs and ideas that can help. . . .
> On the other hand, many women unionists
> have shouldered their share and more of
> the responsibilities of union leader-
> ship. . . . Why have they been able to

do this? . . . Through learning how and
why they have made time for their union
activities, we may learn how to make it
easier for others to do so too. . . .

The cooperating unions are listed below in the order
of their percentage of women members.

1. New York Metro Area Postal Union (formerly
Manhattan-Bronx Postal Union), a union of federal workers
affiliated with the American Postal Workers Union, where
the impact of civil service has equalized the work roles
of men and women: 25 percent of the members are women.
2. Local 342, Amalgamated Meat Cutters and Retail
Food Store Employees, a union where the men are butchers
and managers while the women are meat wrappers, cashiers,
or bookkeepers: 30 percent female membership.
3. Local 463, International Union of Electrical
Workers, a machine and instrument local made up of a number of small factories producing parts for car radios and
other electrical equipment: 35 percent of the members
are women.
4. Local 1597, Custodial Assistants, a local affiliated with District Council 37 of the American Federation
of State, County, and Municipal Employees. Its members
work for the city of New York, cleaning office buildings,
mainly at night: 40 percent of Local 1597 members are
female.
5. United Store Workers, affiliated with Retail,
Wholesale, and Department Store Union. The men and women
of this union work at Bloomingdales and Gimbels: 80 percent of the union's members are women.
6. Local 1199, National Union of Hospital and Health
Care Employees, affiliated with the Retail, Wholesale, and
Department Store Union, whose members work in voluntary
hospitals throughout the metropolitan area. This study
focuses on the blue-collar workers in one of these hospitals. With a Hospital Division membership almost 90 percent female, this union was one of two in the study that
had so few men responding to the questionnaire survey
that data were reliable only as they applied to the women
members.
7. Local 22, Dressmakers' Union, International
Ladies' Garment Workers' Union, is the other union studied
which had so few male respondents that data from men could
not be included. Approximately 90 percent of Local 22's
members are women, and in this respect, it is typical of
the many garment locals in the New York area.

37

Because the local unions in the study represent such a wide variety of industries, each differs in many ways from the others. In two respects, however, they are similar: No matter what the percentage of women members, each is guided and governed primarily by men; where women are active and have moved into key staff or elected posts, it is often at great personal sacrifice.

In the next few pages we shall introduce the reader to those seven unions and set forth some study findings common to them. Tables 3.1 to 3.11 are included in the latter part of the chapter to permit a comparison of the study unions so that differences as well as similarities can be seen at a glance.

NEW YORK METRO AREA POSTAL UNION

Nine out of every ten of the 6,000 women employed in New York City post office stations begin work at either five or six o'clock in the evening, or at midnight. Women are newcomers to the modern postal service, and as newcomers, they work the less popular shifts. While a majority of the men in this union have been members for at least 10 years, only 11 percent of the women have belonged that long (Table 3.11). The entry-level shift for new workers in the postal civil service is the night "tour."

All jobs open to men in the postal system are now open to women. The postal union is one of the two unions in the study where men and women hold jobs at the same skill level; 85 percent are semiskilled. It is the only union where men and women report almost identical educational levels: Over 60 percent are high school graduates, and almost 20 percent of both men and women have education beyond that (Table 3.3).

Women may be newcomers to today's automated postal service, but they are far from newcomers in post office work. Anne Franklin became postmistress of Boston in 1756, the first woman to hold public office in the American colonies. Baltimore had a postmistress in 1775, and Charlestown in 1786. In 1794 the dangerous job of cross-country courier was opened to women, and by 1893 there were 6,335 postmistresses in the United States.[1]

When so many occupations in eighteenth- and nineteenth-century America were closed to them, how did women happen to find their way into the postal service? Arthur Summerfield explains it this way:

this service was essentially a "home service." Except for a few large centers the
postmaster carried out his responsibilities from his house or . . . the building
in which he both kept store and raised his
family. . . . Every member of a postmaster's family was involved in running his
postal affairs. . . . Mail was sorted for
delivery as soon as it arrived. Mail was
accepted when deposited. . . . Provision
had to be made for feeding and "refresh-
ment" of horses and drivers, and this
meant kitchen work. Putting up drivers
and riders overnight added innkeeping to
the postal chores. This was woman's work.
Hence women automatically came into the
postal picture almost from the dawn of the
service. In the postal field, probably
first of all, there came a recognition
that women could be trusted with responsibilities.[2]

Today some 110,000 women work for the postal service.
About 40 percent of the nation's 32,000 post offices are
reported headed by women. Where only 370 women were mail
carriers in 1965, now there are more than 3,500, and an
estimated 50 percent of the distribution clerks are female.[3]

Trade unions in the postal system have been author-
ized under federal law only since 1912, and then they were
restricted to mere consultation accompanied by a long and
unsatisfactory complaint procedure. Postal workers came
to rely on congressional lobbying for improvement in pay
or working conditions. No written contracts spelled out
grievance procedure.

Union recognition came with Executive Order 10988,
issued in 1962 by President John F. Kennedy. The order
provided that the 1 union among the 10 competing organizations that won majority support among postal workers could
get "exclusive" recognition as bargaining agent. The two
largest postal unions were the National Association of
Letter Carriers (NALC) and the United Federation of Postal
Clerks.

In representation elections the United Federation of
Postal Clerks won exclusive recognition at the national
level in 14 of the 15 postal regions, but in the New York
City area it did not. Here exclusive recognition was won

by the Manhattan-Bronx Postal Union, and it was this large local, now known as the New York Metro Area Postal Union, that accepted the invitation to be one of the seven study unions.

Headed by Morris (Moe) Biller, who began as a night tour postal worker on the Lower East Side back in the Depression, New York Metro Area Postal Union with its 26,000 members is the largest postal local in the country. Today it is a part of the new (1971) American Postal Workers Union AFL-CIO, a merger of the five largest postal unions. In this new union, Biller holds the additional post of regional coordinator of the Union Eastern Region, including New York City and New England.

Of special importance to the women in the union is the active encouragement that President Biller has given to women's participation. Of the union's 300 stewards, some 45 are women. Early in 1974, three active women stewards were elected members of the union's Board of Officers, bringing the total to four women on this key board. The Board of Officers is composed of the 25 elected members who hold the post of field officer, a position equivalent to that of business representative, a paid staff position in other unions. In the postal union, however, the field officer is a rank and file worker who settles grievances during working hours without loss of pay.

None of the union's top officers is a woman.

The "Newcomers"

Eleanor Bailey is a good example of the militant rank and file woman in the New York Metro Area Postal Union. Part-time human relations director for the Local, now a field officer with a special interest in legislation, she also works the midnight to 8 a.m. tour five nights a week. Like many women active in their unions, she fits her union activities into her life by cutting back on sleep.

In 1964, when jobs in the post office began to open to women, Bailey entered the postal service. Until then there had been two separate registers, one for men, one for women. The postmaster was free to choose workers from either list. The Kennedy administration integrated the two lists into one. This integration, plus civil service testing for each job, meant that women and blacks had access to post office work without fear of discrimination.

The strike of postal workers in 1970 thrust Bailey into the forefront of union rank and file leadership.

When her shop steward crossed the picket line during the walkout, Bailey challenged him, forcing a recall on his election. She won the post of steward and has continued to be active in the union ever since.

Special Problems of Women Members

The high turnover of the women who work in the post office reflects the difficult work conditions of the job--weekend assignments, late tours, and the necessity for work on holidays. Women have particular problems with post office rules on absences. If a worker is absent three or four times, she can be put on notice. Since 53 percent of the union's women respondents are the sole support of their households, and 65 percent of all women respondents indicate they have children under the age of 18, the problem is readily apparent.

At the suggestion of the union's president, Bailey once conducted a survey to determine child care needs of members. She discovered that some women were forced to leave their children alone while they worked the 3 p.m. to midnight tour. There were close to 600 families stating a need for child care services. Of all the unions in the study, the members of this one most keenly want 24-hour child care centers.

The women in the postal union tend to be young. Over half are below age 35. They have more children under the age of six than do the respondents of the other six study unions. Family responsibilities do, indeed, hold them back from fuller participation in the union. In fact, one of every four responding women indicated that child care would be needed if she were to be more active. One indication that the union is aware of this need is that posted on union bulletin boards are the names of retired members who would like to work as baby-sitters.

LOCAL 342, AMALGAMATED MEAT CUTTERS' AND RETAIL FOOD STORE EMPLOYEES' UNION

The meat you purchase at supermarkets in Long Island, Queens, Brooklyn, or Staten Island is cut and wrapped by members of Local 342, Amalgamated Meat Cutters' and Retail Food Store Employees' Union. This local union has contracts covering 13,000 workers in more than 2,000 stores, which include all major supermarket chains from Staten

Island to Montauk Point. Part-time workers, often students, make up a third of the Local's membership. Approximately 30 percent of the members are women, and more than half of them are part time.

Retail food store workers constitute a textbook case of the type of sharp division between male and female jobs that exists in many industries. The meat cutters--all male--train for two and a half years to become butchers; butchers' pay reflects this, averaging $200 a week or more. Women in the industry are meat wrappers, cashiers, check-out clerks, and bookkeepers, jobs which, for the most part, can be learned in a few days. The union has fought for and won a good pay scale for the kind of work the women do, but their jobs are semiskilled at best and their wages average about $2,000 a year less than the men's.

Women have always been employed in food stores, usu-ally as cashiers, produce clerks, or in dairy departments. But it was not until the emergence of supermarkets that women came into the industry in any numbers. From 1936 on, women moved into the new occupations of meat wrapping and check-out cashier.

Although Local 342 was founded in 1920, the history that concerns us here began some 16 years ago. In 1958 a sluggish, unresponsive and undemocratic Local 342 was put under a trusteeship arrangement by its parent International, the Amalgamated Meat Cutters and Butcher Workmen of North America. A wide-sweeping program of reform was instituted.

Wages and working conditions were improved; members were included in the drawing up of contract demands; and they gained the right to approve or reject contracts. Each member received a copy of the collective bargaining agreement; regular audits were conducted; union posts were filled by secret ballot voting. A bimonthly newspaper was begun to inform members about union affairs. This program, though far from radical, was a complete turnabout for Local 342.

Education Programs Revitalize the Union

The number-one question for the union's new leaders was how to activate the membership. The answer lay in a program of education, and the union utilized every re-source at its disposal: its own international education department, Cornell's School of Industrial and Labor Re-lations, and such training institutes as Harvard's school for union leaders and the AFL-CIO Labor Studies Center.

Training and education programs have been offered staff, officers, Executive Board members, stewards, and the union's rank and file. As Local 342 president, Nickolas Abondolo, once commented: "There are some who have jokingly said we are trying to turn the union into one big classroom. In fact, there is more truth than jest in this."[4]

The effect was to change the entire character of the Local, promoting intensive involvement of members and inspiring a broad program of union services: blood bank, credit union, safety program, pre- and postretirement programs, a senior citizen's organization, and a deep commitment to member education. Through its Apprenticeship Training School, the Local successfully broke the color barrier, placing substantial numbers of minority group members as butchers for the first time.

The Local's leaders have uniformly supported the rank and file thrust of these programs: Nickolas Abondolo, president, who belongs to a younger generation of union official; Irving Stern, director of organization for the Local, who also holds the posts of regional director and vice-president of the international union; Secretary-Treasurer Moe Fliss, who is the oldest of the union's officers and recalls working 85 hours a week for eight dollars during the Depression; George Favale, executive vice-president, a meat cutter at the age of 17, who now heads the political action program of the Local and directs its Long Island activities.

Some Problems Facing the Local

Industry Trends

Early advances in the marketing field brought women into the industry, but today's movement toward automation in meat cutting and pricing is likely to reduce job opportunities. Central meat cutting and packaging means union members will be shifted to central warehouses, and fewer such jobs will be available in the retail stores. It is expected that one day all pricing will be computerized and that the result may be fewer jobs for checkers.

Involving Women in the Union

In a Local where men constitute a majority of the members and also hold all the skilled, status jobs, progress toward equal involvement and equal job opportunity is slow.

43

Women Unionists Are Getting Vocal

"There's got to be more to a job than wrapping meat all day." The Local's officers are taking the complaint seriously.

Women are encouraged to participate in union committees and to serve as shop stewards. Nevertheless, there are only 55 women stewards out of a total of 500. A total of 9 women sits on the 44-member Executive Board. Women are more involved on the political action and legislation committees where 45 of 175 committee members are female. A Women's Division in the Local was established to encourage greater participation of women.

There is increasing pressure from the women for more of their number to be appointed to the union's staff. The only woman staff member at present is Thelma King, assistant director of the Local's safety program. A meat wrapper for 21 years, she is a member of the Local's Executive Board and served as a volunteer safety instructor for six years before being appointed to her full-time staff post in 1973.

Women also are asking the union to make it possible for them to move out of dead-end jobs. As one meat wrapper wrote:

> There should be something more for women . . . there is no place for a woman to go after learning to wrap a piece of meat, and there has to be. Life becomes very dull. What I know now I learned in only three weeks, speed and all. There should be more to it, more responsibility, some mental work. Something has to be done. The pay is good, but without some mental work you get nothing.[5]

Local 342 has responded by awarding union scholarships to women, in proportions far in excess of their membership, to Cornell's two-year Labor/Liberal Arts program. The scholarships are viewed as evidence of the importance attached by the union officers to leadership training for women.

Part-Time Workers

The Meat Cutters' and the United Store Workers' are the two unions in the study with substantial numbers of

44

part-time workers under contract. In Local 342, the presence of students as part-time workers accounts for the
fact that one in every four women members in the Local is
under the age of 25. It probably influences the education
level as well; this is the only union where women show a
substantially higher educational level than the men. Furthermore, Local 342 has more unmarried women members than
any other union in the study, and we may assume that the
part-time student workers explain this figure.

The number of part-time workers presents a special
problem to the Local. These members are covered by the
contract and receive the same benefits, prorated, that
full-time workers do. But because of the responsibilities
that keep them out of the full-time work force, they are
not active in the life of the union and have been consistently hard to involve.

Job Satisfaction

Of the men in this union, 89.6 percent hold skilled
jobs. The number of women who do is statistically invis-
ible. The wide gap in job satisfaction, consequently, is
not surprising. In the "slightly dissatisfied" category,
men and women in this union show the widest gap of any of
the seven study unions. Skilled workers tend to be satisfied with their work. In view of the educational level of
women members relative to the skill level of their work,
we might assume special job disaffection. Harder to explain is the fact that almost an identical number of men
and woman responds that they "enjoy" their jobs. Examin-
ing the less-than-satisfied figures, however, we find that
only 22.5 percent of the men were in any way dissatisfied
with their work, while 38 percent of the women either dis-
liked their jobs or were somewhat dissatisfied.

LOCAL 463, INTERNATIONAL UNION
OF ELECTRICAL WORKERS

This local union of 2,500 members is known as an
"amalgamated" local within a large industrial parent union
of some 300,000 men and women who work in the electrical
industry. While most Locals affiliated with the International Union of Electrical, Radio, and Machine Workers
(IUE) are organized in one large plant, Local 463 has
contracts with 36 plants ranging in size from 4 employees

to 650. Its members produce electronic parts, head sets, and auto parts and equipment. About 40 percent of Local 463 members are women; this is roughly the same proportion belonging to the IUE nationally (35 percent).

Background--the IUE

During and following World War II, women entered and remained in the electrical manufacturing industry and its union. They have been represented on the International Union's Executive Board since 1956 (though today there are still only two women on this board). However, in 1972, a convention resolution was adopted that the IUE establish a Women's Council. Mary Callahan was elected chairperson of this council by representatives appointed to it from each IUE District and Conference Board.

The IUE Constitution reads: "The chairman of the Women's Council shall participate with and advise the Executive Board on all matters following within the jurisdiction of the Women's Council" (Article XXIII, Section B).

The IUE showed an early concern for integrating women into the life of the union, and today is one of the few internationals to survey its membership in order to learn what posts women hold in the local unions and how involved the Locals are in issues of concern to women members.

The first nationwide survey carried out, in 1965, indicated that women, if they held local office at all, tended to be stewards, local secretaries, or trustees. This was not enough. To develop more women leaders, the union urged each Local to form a Social Action Committee to provide new channels for women's participation; women were specifically encouraged to join.

A second survey two years later showed a small but definite increase in the number of women holding posts as union officers. In addition, more women were being selected to attend District Council meetings (the union is divided into seven geographical districts) and union conventions.

The IUE has developed one of the strongest equal-opportunity programs in the country to support its Policy Statement on Equal Employment: "Local unions should regard Title VII of the Civil Rights Act as a means of forcing recalcitrant employers to cooperate fully with the IUE in achieving its historic commitment of equality for all."

The union's affirmative action program involves its legal department (where the associate counsel is a woman

deeply committed to this program) and its Education and
Women's Activities Department, where Director Gloria Johnson encourages the Social Action Committees and champions
the cause of union women in the IUE.

In March 1973, the IUE Executive Board unanimously
adopted a resolution outlining "a coordinated and detailed
program throughout the entire union" to eliminate all remaining vestiges of race and sex discrimination. Check
lists were developed to help Locals determine if any such
discrimination existed either in plant practices or in
contract language.

Gloria Johnson sees many reasons for the measurable
increase in activity of women members. She attributes it
in part to a heightened awareness of the issues by both
men and women through publicity of the equal-employment
litigation pursued by the union and the landmark decisions
the union has secured on cases dealing with pregnancy,
maternity, and equal pay. Eliminating separate seniority
lists has enabled women to move into jobs previously held
exclusively by men. Women members have been asking more
questions and are less hesitant to accept union committee
posts or run for office. Finally, the union is fighting
for specific women's demands as part of its basic collective bargaining program: disability for pregnancy-related
illnesses, maternity as a disability, and substantial
women's representation in the skilled trades council and
in apprenticeship programs.

In spite of all this, a wage differential remains
between the earnings of men and women members, and the
union is fighting to eliminate it. Equal pay is the rule
for equal work, but most women in the world of work still
find themselves with unequal work and lower-paying jobs.

"Women need to know what the union is doing for them
and then they get more involved," says Johnson. She feels
women are responding directly to the union's affirmative
program for equal rights, and to the Women's Conference,
sponsored by the districts and by the international office.
"Women, especially minority women, are playing an increasingly more active role in their unions," she reports.

Local 463

Within this framework, let us take a closer look at
Local 463, which was founded by James Trenz some 23 years
ago when it separated from the United Electrical Workers
after the latter was expelled from the Congress of

Industrial Organizations. The Local decided to join
forces with the new IUE in 1951 and has been an amalgamated Local within this union since then.

As in the industry nationally, women entered electrical manufacturing plants in the New York area during
the World War II years. Local 463 president James Trenz
reports that women work in most of the 36 plants under
contract, but more of them work in low-skill rather than
high-skill jobs. Few women are part-timers in this Local.
Only a small number of sheet metal factories and machine
shops have no women at all.

Jim Trenz is proud of the Local's civil rights record.
In the largest shop under contract, Local 463 broke the
color bar. White workers threatened to walk out if blacks
were hired. Trenz said, "Go ahead. If you strike, you'll
have no union backing." Nothing happened, and there has
been no trouble on this score ever since.

Women in Local 463

Today two of the Local's four top elected officers
are women: Vice-President Edith Hammer and Treasurer
Bernice Cattrell. Edith Hammer recalls the struggles of
organizing the radio parts plant where she worked, back
in 1933. "Our first strike lasted 12 weeks, and we lost.
But two years later we were out again, this time for 18
weeks, and this time we won." She became a steward, then
shop chairman, and has served the IUE as a staff representative for 25 years.

Discussing the fact that she never married, Hammer
said, "In those days what man would want to be married to
a woman who traveled all the time and was out at meetings
every night?" Like many women leaders of that period and
earlier, the union has been her life. "I have loved my
work, every minute of it," she asserts.

Women hold at least 25 of the 80 shop steward posts
in the Local, and 4 women are shop chairmen. All plant
openings are posted, and bidding for them is by seniority,
which is shopwide. While women are free to bid on traditionally male jobs, such as punch press operator, they do
not do so very often. The skilled jobs are consistently
held by men, and women tend to find themselves on assembly
line and piece-work operations. Most apprentices are men.
There is little upward mobility as yet for the women,
though some has occurred, for example, in Die Setter and
Lead classifications.

48

Because the jobs held by women tend to be tedious, Trenz notes, turnover is higher than for men, but that is changing. "Younger women are coming into the industry, and they come in to stay, even when they have small children. Financial pressures are heavy on families these days."

Of the seven unions cooperating in the study, questionnaires show Local 463 members have the highest married rate of all (63 percent of the women, 80 percent of the men); members also tend to be among the highest in the study in the number of children they have (Table 3.6). One in four Local 463 women is divorced, widowed, or separated, and 45 percent of all women report that they are the sole support of their families.

Trenz finds that the collective-bargaining concerns of the members tend to reflect these figures and differ according to sex. Men seem more interested in pay and pensions, women in sick leave, holidays, and vacations.

Steward training classes and committees such as the Political Action, Civil Rights, and Negotiating Committee provide several avenues of activity for interested members. Meeting attendance is a special concern of the Local, but its biggest problem centers around a net loss of jobs due to imports. In 1972, for example, this small Local lost four plants through closings.

CUSTODIAL ASSISTANTS, LOCAL 1597

One of the reasons New York City's skyline is so bright at night is that women like Agnes Johnson are moving from office to office in municipal buildings emptying ashtrays, dusting, and sweeping long after the office workers have left. Agnes Johnson is typical of the custodial assistants who belong to Local 1597, a union whose 2,600 members are affiliated with District Council 37 (DC 37) of the American Federation of State, County, and Municipal Employees (AFSCME). This local union was chosen for the study to represent blue-collar employees of the city.

District Council 37

Under the leadership of District Director Victor Gotbaum, DC 37 has grown from a union of a few hundred city employees to its present size of more than 100,000.

A man of great vitality and community conscience, Gotbaum
is involved in numerous civic and labor posts, but DC 37
has first claim on his time and energies. He is proud of
its rapid growth and especially of the range of services
it affords its members. One of his concerns about the
union's growth is that it not get bureaucratic in its big-
ness, and as he oversees the 62 local unions and six major
divisional units of the organization, he seeks to ensure
that this will not happen.

The major divisional units of DC 37 are Clerical-
Administrative, Hospital, Professional, School, White-
Collar, and Blue-Collar. It is to this last that Local
1597 belongs. Over 56,000 of DC 37's members are women,
half of them in the Clerical-Administrative Division.
Only 1,400 women are in its Blue-Collar Division, and almost all of these are in the custodial assistants' Local.

Although none of the division directors is female,
two assistant directors are. Two department heads (Personal Services and Surgical Consultations) are women, and
in two other departments women hold the positions of
assistant director. The District 37 associate counsel is
also a woman. Of the union's staff of 100, about one-
third are female.

An extensive network of programs, benefits, and services is available to DC 37 members. These include, among
others, medical plans with optical, dental, and drug benefits, an excellent pension plan, summer camp programs for
1,500 children, a weekly information radio program, a retiree program open to its 8,000 retired members, and an
excellent career development and training program.

This last is a tribute to the vision of Lillian
Roberts, associate director of DC 37, and reflects her
knowledge of the membership's strong desire for education
and upward mobility. All day and into the night the
union's education department conducts classes. More than
6,000 members a year enroll. The students train for promotional exams, prepare for high school equivalency tests
(over 3,000 have taken this program), or study to become
licensed practical nurses (some 1,000 former nurses' aides
have achieved this through the union's program).

Upward movement is the theme. In 1971, for example,
when a supervisory clerk test was coming up, the union
ran a preparatory program on television. More than 12,000
members trooped to the union hall for the necessary texts
and materials to take this course via their home TV sets.

Tuition refunds have been negotiated by the union as
part of collective bargaining agreements with the city,

and members can attend college right in their union's
headquarters while holding down full-time jobs during the
daytime.

Leadership in DC 37

Second in command to District Council's dynamic
director, Victor Gotbaum, is one of the country's out-
standing women union leaders, Associate Director Lillian
Roberts. A former hospital worker from the Chicago ghetto,
she grew up knowing welfare during a period when relief
supplies arrived in boxes and families on relief were identifiable because they made their dresses from the same
bolts of blue cloth distributed to all. An honors student
in high school, there were no funds to pay college costs;
so Roberts' university scholarship had to be turned down.
Work life began in earnest when she became the first
black nurse's aide ever hired at Chicago's Lying-In Hospital. It was not long before she was elected steward and
learning how to win grievances. The principles for winning that she developed then have served her ever since:
Pick your issues carefully. Do not get divided on ethnic
lines. Keep your mind on the big things. Do your home-
work.
In May 1973, speaking at the AFL-CIO Labor Studies
Center training institute for women staff of unions,
Roberts voiced her thoughts about the women in her union:

> The women in our union are more representa-
> tive of the American Labor Movement of the
> 30s, the hungry, growing years, than they
> are of the Labor Movement today. . . .
> Women in the work force cannot be included
> yet among the self-satisfied . . . they
> aren't there yet. They are still on the
> way up. These are the creative, demand-
> ing, rewarding times of moving up.

Local 1597

Back in 1940 John Crumedy, president of Local 1597,
was the first black "cleaner" at Brooklyn College, and
earned $900 a year. Today Local 1597 members start at
$6,700 with a 10 percent differential for night work.
Salaries range up to $9,000 a year depending on length
of service.

51

When the Local was chartered in 1966, one of the first
demands of members was to change the job title from "cleaners" to "custodial assistants." While salary and job security have always been high-priority issues for the members, dignity has come first. Many of the 1,100 women
members of Local 1597 are former household workers; almost
all are black or Hispanic American, as are the men.

Over half of all the women members (54 percent, according to union figures) work a night shift, 30-hour week.
Benefits and salary are prorated accordingly. Today, one
of the key problems in the Local is centered on these workers and the extra work demanded of them resulting from the
city's job freeze. Custodial assistants are not replaced,
and the 30-hour workers feel that they are asked to accomplish the work formerly done by 40-hour teams. The union
is seeking agreement from the city to give the 30-hour
women the option of moving into the 40-hour category, with
its added pay, before appointments are made from examination lists being developed for the city program of putting
welfare recipients to work.

Another problem for Local 1597 members is the limited
number of opportunities for upgrading. A recent breakthrough gave custodial assistants the right to train and
take the examination for laborer, a position starting at
about $11,000 a year. To help members prepare for this
test, entirely physical in nature, the union organized
centers in four boroughs, duplicated test equipment, and
provided training opportunities. At least one Local 1597
woman passed this test and is now awaiting appointment.
If she gets the job, she will be the first woman to move
into a city laborer job through a promotional exam. Typing classes and high school equivalency programs are also
especially valued by members of this Local.

A third major problem is job attrition. As custodial
assistants leave their jobs, the city hires outside cleaning firms. Over the last several years, the number of
Local 1597 members doing the actual cleaning of city
buildings has dropped from 1,600 to 700 (other members of
the Local run elevators and serve as watchmen or atten-
dants).

Women in Local 1597

Two of the Local's elected officers are women, and
four women sit on the seven-member Executive Board (one
as vice-president, one as recording secretary, two as

52

trustees). However, just 10 of the Local's 40 stewards
are women.

Women custodial assistants differ markedly from women
of the six other study unions. They tend to be considerably older and to have older children (Tables 3.2 and 3.7).
Although most of the women have few children, a higher
number than in other unions has large families (Table 3.6).
A total of 52 percent, however, reports that their children
are over 18 years in age, compared to only 26 percent of
the men. The men tend to be younger than the women in this
union and also to hold two jobs.

This is the union with the highest percentage of women
who are the sole support of their households--62 percent.
While the men in the Local are likely to be married (71
percent), the women tend to be single or formerly married
(59 percent).

Women respondents have had more formal education than
the men: 77 percent have gone beyond eighth grade compared to 69 percent of the men. This is somewhat greater
than that of the national labor force in general, where
5.6 percent more women than men have gone beyond the
eighth grade.

Men are somewhat more satisfied with their jobs than
are the women, and the union relates this finding to the
fact that men have traditionally had more opportunities
to advance--to posts such as foreman. This may change,
however, as separate lines for men and women have not been
abolished. Not many months ago promotional examinations
for the position of junior building custodian were posted,
and 275 members of the Local enrolled in the union class
to prepare for the test. About 70 percent of the students
were reportedly women.

UNITED STORE WORKERS' UNION, LOCALS 2 AND 3

The 11,000 members and 1,000 retirees of this union
represent the only white-collar Local in the study, although they are by no means higher in the pay scale than
the other Locals surveyed (women members average about
$133 a week). A union whose parent international is the
Retail, Wholesale, and Department Store Union (RWDSU),
its members work at Gimbels, Bloomingdales, and branch
stores of these chains, as well as at several smaller department stores in the city. Only Bloomingdales (3,300
members) and the two Gimbels stores (4,000 members) in
Manhattan were included in the study.

A total of 80 percent of the union's members is women.

Background

Department store employees began organizing in the depths of the Depression. A small band of workers, including present president William Michelson, looked for a union to help them fight long hours, low pay, and job insecurity. With their victory following a 13-week strike at Ohrbachs in 1934, they were on their way, winning a $16 weekly salary, a five-day week, and the right to arbitrate grievances.

The union grew, especially following the birth of the Congress of Industrial Organizations (CIO) and a sit-down strike in the 5 and 10 cents stores. In 1937, with the first contract at Hearns Department Store, the union came into its own. Gimbels' workers won their first contract in 1939, Bloomingdales and Saks 34th Street employees in 1940, and Sterns' workers in 1942. Each new benefit was hard won: The 40-hour five-day week meant a 21-day strike in 1941. The Security Plan (medical benefits), which Michelson says is the single most important benefit the union offers, was gained in 1949. Pensions came in 1954. The $37\frac{1}{2}$-hour work week was won in 1963, but two years later members had to strike for their new contract at both Bloomingdales and Sterns. More recent gains include higher minimum wages and a cost-of-living clause.

In 1968, the United Store Workers' Union broke away from District 65 when the latter group became an independent union. The Store Workers' retained its affiliation with RWDSU. It has achieved a reputation for union democracy, membership education, and most recently for its breakthrough in opening high-commission selling jobs to women. High-commission jobs—in furniture, appliances, and rugs—traditionally had been held exclusively by men.

The biggest problem the union faces is organizing unorganized store workers. Michelson sees this as a special challenge for the women in the union. He encourages leadership-training programs for women members because he feels the only way to organize department stores (and there are more than 50,000 unorganized store workers in the metropolitan New York area) is for women to reach out to other women. Realistically, he sees expansion of the union's membership as the best route for bringing more women into leadership posts. Presently there is only one woman vice-president in the union. Four other staff posts of ten are held by women (one of them a policy-making position). But with 80 percent of the union's members female, women increasingly desire a greater role.

54

Related Study Findings

Close to half the Store Workers' membership is composed of part-time workers. Many of these members are active and feel very much a part of the union. Their union identity reflects the fact that as salespersons retire, they often continue to work part time in the store. The union plans special meetings during the day for these members to help them stay involved. They are eligible to join all committees and are encouraged to do so.

This is a union of somewhat older workers. Our study, which may reflect the higher interest and questionnaire return of older members, nonetheless shows 62 percent of the respondents over 45 years of age (the national average for women workers is 39 years). This is the union that shows the highest degree of job satisfaction: 77 percent of the women are satisfied or better, 73 percent of the men. This does not surprise union officials, who feel that store workers do indeed like their work, especially the personal contact with the public and one another, and the sense of satisfaction they get from helping customers.

Turnover is low. Today younger women are coming into the industry, where previously it was middle-aged women with grown children who were the mainstay of the stores. Union leaders feel this reflects the economic needs of families as well as the growing number of women who are the sole support of their households (43 percent of women respondents in this union are).

The men in the Store Workers' Union are a far younger group than the women and tend to be single (40 percent as opposed to 21 percent of the women). Both men and women in this union have the highest education level of all respondents in the study unions, with 82 percent of the men having gone beyond high school, and 80 percent of the women (see Table 3.3).

There is a big gap in skill level between men and women workers in this union: 91 percent of the women hold semiskilled jobs compared to only 50 percent of the men. This is slowly changing as women are encouraged by the union to bid for commission jobs.

One of the problems the union seeks to overcome through its education program is that most of its shop stewards and program participants are older members. Over three-fourths of its women stewards and two-thirds of its men stewards are over 45 years of age.

The union is asking how it can reach its younger members more effectively. Security Plan Director Eleanor

Tilson, together with other staff members, has taken on the responsibility of developing special programs for women members. The programs aim at building women's self-confidence and leadership skill and increasing their participation in the union. Tilson has worked with Cornell's trade union women's program in designing special classes for women members. She hopes to launch a new training program to develop their organizing skills and interests. Vice-President Ida Torres, Organizer Gloria Ford, and Union Editor Doris Loewi have all been active in this long-range effort. It is primarily because of their work that women have been encouraged to bid for commission jobs and have been strengthened to face the competitiveness that accompanies these jobs.

A New Philosophy

Michelson voices his sharp concern about the need to increase the participation of women members this way:

> This organizing of unorganized store workers won't happen until a new social force develops in the industry. The solution must be related to questions bothering women in the industry. We have already learned that economic differences between union and nonunion standards are not sufficient incentives for nonunion workers. We must design a program to provide conditions over and beyond wages, hours, working conditions, and job security. It has to be the counterpart to the Civil Rights movement among the women in this industry.

DISTRICT 1199, NATIONAL UNION OF HOSPITAL AND HEALTH CARE EMPLOYEES

The 15-story modern union headquarters, new in 1970 and already outgrown, bustles summer and winter with classes and meetings. It is a far cry from the $30 a month loft where the union began, some 42 years ago, as an organization of registered pharmacists and drugstore workers. Today District 1199 is the heart of a new National Union of Hospital and Health Care Employees,

89,000 strong, whose contracts cover workers in 313 insti-
tutions in 15 states and the District of Columbia. During
1973, members were added at the rate of a thousand a month.
The union's goal is to increase its membership to 100,000
by the end of 1974.

The district is the fulcrum of the new national union.
Many out-of-town districts bear the 1199 number but have a
letter attached, as District 1199 C (Philadelphia), District 1199 E (Baltimore), District 1199 Mass. (Massachu-
setts). Administratively, District 1199, which represents
61,500 members in New York, New Jersey, and Connecticut,
includes three divisions: hospital workers, pharmacists,
and guild members (licensed practical nurses, social workers, technicians, office workers, and others in hospital
and health care facilities). Although it is a new national union, it retains its affiliation with its present
international--the Retail, Wholesale, and Department Store
Union (RWDSU).

Background

It was in 1959 that the 5,000-member union of pharmacists launched an organizing drive to unionize workers in
voluntary hospitals. Hospital employees were earning not
quite $30 a week for 44 to 48 hours of work and were ex-
cluded from federal and state legislated floors for wages
or ceilings on hours.

The drive succeeded, but only after struggles which
included strikes both in 1959 and 1962. Workers at University Hospital, the hospital selected to represent District 1199 in our study, won their first contract in 1964.
Today most major voluntary hospitals in the city are under
contract with District 1199, and hospital workers earn a
minimum of $151 a week (June 1974). The workers have a
medical plan that includes dental care and prescription
drugs, six weeks' disability leave for maternity, and a
good pension program. There are children's camp and college scholarship programs, cultural, social, and educational activities, a credit union, and a model retiree
program. Currently the union is sponsoring a low- and
middle-income cooperative housing project.

In speaking of 1199, Moe Foner, executive secretary,
emphasizes that it is an organization that has always
"linked its economic struggles with the fight for human
rights." Dr. Martin Luther King, Jr., often called 1199
his favorite labor union, and it is his widow, Coretta
Scott King, who serves as honorary chairperson of the
national union.

Training and Upgrading

Perhaps the pride of the union is its training and upgrading program. Funded through a 1 percent tax on net payroll paid by the 65 hospitals that are members of the League of Voluntary Hospitals, union members can move through three levels of education: (1) study for high school equivalency certificates, on their own time at the union hall, (2) tuition assistance for up to six semester hours of college work a term, (3) full-time study with 80 percent of salary reimbursed for one to two years, leading to an associate in applied science (graduating registered nurses).

Workers can move up through this program. Licensed practical nurses become registered nurses (RN); nurses' aides become licensed practical nurses; orderlies, porters, dishwashers, and laundry workers become X-ray, laboratory, and surgical technicians. It was an 1199er, Joanna Domanico of Long Island Jewish Hospital, studying in the union's program toward her RN, who correctly suggested that a boy's paralysis was caused by a tick bite, while doctors were puzzling over a diagnosis.

The Challenges: Organizing, Leadership

Since only 11 percent of this country's 3.5 million hospital and health care workers are in unions today, organizing is what the union sees as its principal task, and not an easy one. As recently as August 1972, an 1199 organizer was shot and killed by a private guard during a Philadelphia organizing strike.

Another key challenge, according to Leon Davis, president of the union since its inception, is securing and developing leadership. He believes that women will share increasingly in the union's leadership--they are 70 percent of the total membership and perhaps 90 percent of its Hospital Division. Today three women are vice-presidents on the new national union's Executive Board of 18, and another, Doris Turner, is a general officer. Turner is secretary of the national union, executive vice-president of District 1199, and director of its Hospital Division.

Davis feels that black women, who make up the majority of the union's membership, are the future of the union. But the union demands a lot from its staff and has trouble filling staff posts from among active rank and file. A member tapped for such a position, if he or she is willing

to try it, can get a one-year leave of absence for a trial
period. There is little financial lure, the hours are
long and the work demanding. There is little time for
family life. Davis comments: "A person must really love
the work to take it on."

Doris Turner, a leader in the Lenox Hill Hospital
workers' strike back in 1959, recognizes that women make
many sacrifices for the union as rank and file leaders.
There are countless meetings they are called on to attend.
As she says, "A relationship of deep trust must exist between husband and wife if a woman is to be really active
in 1199." In her own case, she reports, it has meant that
others have had more of a hand in bringing up her children
than she has.

Women in 1199

This Local's women members are the youngest among the
seven study unions. The largest group (42 percent) is between the ages of 25 and 35, and only 23 percent are over
45. Compared to the other unions, the women have a somewhat lower education level, with 54 percent having "completed some high school, or less." Only among garment
workers, a much older group, have fewer members reported
completing high school (see Table 3.3). However, 20 percent of District 1199 respondents indicate they are taking
courses, and over half of the women believe they can advance or be upgraded--a direct reflection of the union's
training and upgrading program, whose participants are
overwhelmingly female.

Only one union, the Electrical Workers, has a higher
percentage of married women. More District 1199 women
have children between the ages of 6 and 18 than in any
other study union. They are second highest in having
children under age six (see Table 3.7).

Some 60 percent of 1199 respondents indicate that
they are the sole support of their families (only custodial assistant women show a higher proportion, 62 percent). Hospital workers also show a lower pattern of interrupted work histories than women in any of the other
unions: 75 percent indicate that they have always worked.
Only the garment union, with a somewhat higher percentage
of single women, shows more respondents who have always
worked (76 percent).

Most hospital workers are unskilled--69 percent; 31
percent indicate that they are semiskilled. However, this

is the only union where <u>no</u> respondents whatsoever checked "dislike job." The general level of job satisfaction is very high; 71 percent, the highest percentage of all unions, checked the category "well satisfied" (see Table 3.10).

Perhaps the high job satisfaction relates to the amount of contact with others during the day's work and the nature of that contact. These workers also are able to see their job through from beginning to end and to control their work--both in pace and quality.[6] If the job is done well, the satisfaction belongs to the individual and to no one else.

LOCAL 22, INTERNATIONAL LADIES' GARMENT WORKERS' UNION

The oldest of the seven unions in our study, the Dressmakers' Union Local 22, rose out of the sweatshops to become, at one time, one of the largest Locals in the International Ladies' Garment Workers' Union (ILGWU). The dress industry developed later than many of the "ready-mades," because women were willing to purchase at retail the skirts and blouses they wore during a period when they continued to have their dresses made to order. By the 1920s, however, this had changed. One interesting hold-over from the earlier practice is that, for 90 percent or more of Local 22 members, each worker still makes the entire dress. This is quite different from the line system in most garment plants. It may account for the high level of job satisfaction among the members of this union, but it also makes for a key problem: the decline of the dress industry in New York. Factories are moving out of town, and retail stores are buying dresses that cost less because they are made on line systems in largely nonunion plants in the South and the Southwest.

Background

Before the days of the ILGWU, garment workers labored from 7:30 in the morning to 9:00 at night in "high" season, with no overtime. Sometimes they worked seven days a week, and management posted signs that read: "If you don't come in on Sunday, don't come in on Monday."

Pauline Newman, old-time ILGWU organizer, recalls that management might give workers a small five-cent pie as overtime pay. The shops were firetraps, and she

remembers the broken stairs, the gas jets, the pot-bellied
stove in the middle of the room. Only the finishers were
warm in winter, since they sat near the stove. But in
summer the crowded shops were ovens. Toilets were in the
yards, and scraps of fabric, oiled rags, and waste paper
piled up in the aisles between the machines. In busy season, workers sometimes slept in the factories on piles of
cloth because there was not time to get home, sleep a few
hours, and get back to work without being late.

In the early part of the twentieth century, many
workers still had to buy their own machines--about half of
them carried their machines with them from job to job.
All workers were responsible for machine repair, for thread,
oil, and needles. Often they were charged (and overcharged)
for the electricity that ran their machines. It is this
industry that is notorious for home work. Workers carried
bundles of garments home to finish, with all members of
the family laboring far into the night to make a few extra
pennies.

Into this system came the union, bringing a 40-hour
week and, since 1933, a 35-hour week. Members have a union
health center, the first one in the country, established
in 1913. Since 1937 ILGWU members have had paid vacations
and, since 1943, pensions.

Local 22, originally part of a larger local, dates
its permanent charter from 1927. It has always been a
"gateway" union, offering membership to immigrants and
newcomers to the city without regard to race, national
origin, or sex. Locals were organized by language at one
time, and cutters in the dress industry, all men, are in
a separate Local even today. Local 22 today is predominantly female and has so few men among its members that
our study questionnaires were tabulated only for the
women. Most of the women work at making the garments,
but some are pressers, examiners, or cleaners.

One of the biggest problems--and it is one cause of
the relatively low wages in the industry today--is the
large number of unorganized shops in other parts of the
country. It is said that the union could probably triple
its membership if these plants could be organized.

Local 22 Today

From its early position as one of the largest Locals
in the ILGWU, with approximately 28,000 members, Local 22
has shrunk to a membership of 9,300. The Local covers

some 1,600 shops in the New York area. Many of these are still in the same loft buildings where they have been for the last 50 or 60 years. Prices are established for each style of dress by the "piece," and shop chairladies nego- tiate the rate for each style. The chairlady is the back- bone of the union; as Complaints Manager Marie Calera puts it, "They are the eyes of the union in the shop." Senior- ity plays no role in garment plants. There is a share- the-work philosophy so that if the bundles of work are thin, they are divided evenly among all, and everyone works a shorter day or week.

Our study indicates that job satisfaction in this union is the second highest of all seven unions (second to the Store Workers'). Calera explains it this way: "Styles change and there is always the challenge of figur- ing out a better way of sewing the garment. The members are thinking all the time."

A dressmaker says, "When you finish a hard garment and the owner compliments you and says it is beautiful, you're really proud of what you have done."[7] Work condi- tions permit sewing-machine operators to relate to one another, to chat with the woman at the next machine, and to control their own rate of work. If a woman wants to leave a little early one day, she can. In addition, there is often a gap between seasons of as much as two or three weeks, with unemployment insurance cushioning the financial loss, giving women a chance to catch up on their job responsibilities at home.

Local 22 has the highest skill level and the highest average age of any of the seven study unions; 70 percent of the respondents report that they are over 45 years old. Almost three-quarters of those who reported they had chil- dren indicated that the children were over 18 years. Half of the women in the study are the sole support of their families.

This Local remains a miniature United Nations and is proud of the fact that it counts 36 nationalities among its members.

Leadership in the Local

Almost all the top leaders in the Local, as in the ILGWU nationally, are men. In fact, none of the Inter- national's Executive Board members are women, as of this writing, although some 80 percent of the membership is female.

In Local 22, five out of ten business agents are women. The highest position ever held by a woman in the Local was that of Rose Mirsky, a Russian immigrant who came to the United States and, like so many others, took a job as a machine operator in a dress factory. Always active in union-organizing efforts, she became a union staff member in 1932. By the time of her death at the age of 50, in 1948, she had moved up to the twin posts of manager of the Affiliated Department of Better Dresses and manager of the Labor Bureau.

The highest position held by a woman in the Local today is that of complaints manager of the Dress Joint Board, Marie Calera, who handles all breaches of the contract. Organizing meetings for Spanish-speaking workers brought Calera to the forefront of union activity back in 1943. Two years later she spent a summer at the Hudson Shore Labor School and returned to become a business agent for the Local, a post she held for 25 years. In 1971, she was appointed complaints manager for the Dress Joint Board, which includes Local 22. Hungry for education, Calera attended the Cornell Labor/Liberal Arts Program, completed a B.A. degree in labor studies, and is now working toward her M.A. in the field of teaching English as a second language.

Israel Breslow, secretary-manager of the Dressmakers' Union, continues the now-famous art classes begun by Charles Zimmerman, former manager of Local 22. These classes have been oversubscribed for the last 30 years. Much of the union's education program serves a social function, with trips, dances, and weekends at the ILGWU vacation resort, Unity House, in the Pocono Mountains. English language classes and shop steward training are also offered.

Most shop stewards are old-timers, and the Local finds it difficult to get younger women active in the union. Attendance at membership meetings is declining, and most stewards are over 45 years of age. In the expectation of learning more about why this is so, Local 22 joined in the year-long study of the participation of women in the Local.

CHARACTERISTICS OF UNION MEMBERS: DATA COMPARED

The remainder of this chapter compares demographic data from the seven study unions. Incorporated into 12 tables, the data present the ages and marital status of

1,517 rank and file respondents to questionnaires distributed through the seven unions, their education, number of children, work history, skill levels, job satisfaction, length of time in the union, and the way men and women view their chances for advancing on the job. The presentation of data in comparative form serves to highlight the different characteristics of each union as well as their areas of similarity. Table 3.1 shows union size and percent female membership.

TABLE 3.1

Union Size and Percent Female Membership

	Size of Union (number members)	Percent Female
Postal	26,000	25
Meat Cutters	14,000	30*
Electrical	2,500	33
Custodial	2,674	41
Store	12,000	80*
Hospital	1,418†	85‡
Garment	9,300	90

*Leaders indicate the number of part-time women workers is approximately 50 percent of the total female membership. Questionnaire responses, however, represent a smaller proportion of part-timers: for meat cutters, 32 percent of the female responses; for store workers, 35.5 percent.

†In the hospital surveyed (60,000 in New York City).

‡Hospital division only.

Data on respondents are reported as 100 percent; the percent not responding is reported as "No Answer." A copy of the full questionnaire that was used is included as Appendix C. A discussion of the methods of circulating and recovering questionnaires from the rank and file members of the seven unions is part of Appendix A.

Table 3.2 compares the ages of men and women respondents. In a majority of the unions, more than half of the women are over 45, compared to 43 percent of working women in the general population. In only one of the five

TABLE 3.2

Ages of Respondents
(in percents)

	Postal	Meat Cutters	Electrical	Custodial	Store	Hospital	Garment
Under 25							
Men	3.6	12.0	9.7	5.1	17.1	*	*
Women	8.8	26.0	2.1	0.0	12.1	8.3	0.0
25 to 35							
Men	20.9	32.0	20.4	24.1	27.6	*	*
Women	45.6	16.0	12.6	3.1	4.7	41.7	6.7
35 to 45							
Men	20.9	44.0	20.4	23.4	11.8	*	*
Women	24.6	50.0	26.3	25.8	16.8	26.7	23.6
Over 45							
Men	54.7	12.0	49.5	47.4	43.4	*	*
Women	21.1	8.0	58.9	71.1	66.4	23.3	69.7
No answer							
Men	0.0	0.0	1.0	0.0	2.6	*	*
Women	1.7	0.0	1.0	1.0	6.1	4.8	2.2

*Only women members were included in the study.

study unions with male respondents were the majority of the men over 45. Just as the men in our study tend to be younger than the women, so too are male workers in the population as a whole, where only 40 percent are 45 years or older.

The large number of women under 25 years of age in the Meat Cutters' Union reflects the fact that 32 percent of the female respondents work part time. Among store workers, about the same percentage of respondents are part-time workers, but they add to the over-45 age bracket since many retired women are part-time workers.

Only the men in the Meat Cutters' Union approach the national norm (11.9 percent) for men or women workers under 25.

The largest proportions of older women are found in the Custodial Assistants' and Garment Unions, where 71 and 70 percent of the women are over 45 years of age.

The levels of education completed are set forth in Table 3.3. The highest levels are found among the men and women in the Store Workers' and the Postal Unions, with the men reporting a somewhat higher level. It may be of interest for the reader to compare the education of study respondents with the national figures reported in the 1972 Handbook of Labor Statistics, U.S. Department of Labor.

Education Level of the National Labor Force	Men (percent)	Women (percent)
Completed elementary school	15.8	11.5
Completed some high school	16.9	16.4
Completed high school	35.7	45.4
More formal education	14.0	13.9

Respondents with the least formal education are the custodial assistants, men and women, though the women show a somewhat higher level of education than the men. Hospital workers and garment workers are also at the low end. The Meat Cutters' Union is the only one where the women have a substantially higher education level than the men, although 100 percent of the women hold unskilled or semiskilled jobs. However, the part-time workers who are students weight this figure at the high end.

Table 3.4 compares the marital status of respondents. There are significant differences between men and women in almost every category and in every union. The percentage of women who are divorced, widowed, or separated ranges from 24 percent for the Electrical Union to 48

TABLE 3.3

Education Completed
(in percents)

Education Completed	Postal	Meat Cutters	Electrical	Custodial	Store	Hospital	Garment
Elementary or less							
Men	0.7	13.3	4.3	31.4	1.5	*	*
Women	1.8	4.3	9.3	23.3	2.2	20.8	22.5
Some high school							
Men	17.8	35.6	32.3	39.7	13.6	*	*
Women	19.3	34.0	41.9	48.8	11.2	34.0	35.2
Graduated high school							
Men	63.7	46.7	40.9	25.6	43.9	*	*
Women	61.4	42.6	45.3	24.4	56.2	35.8	23.9
More formal education							
Men	17.0	4.4	18.3	1.7	37.9	*	*
Women	17.5	19.1	4.5	3.5	23.6	9.4	15.5
More other kinds							
Men	0.7	0.0	4.3	1.7	3.0	*	*
Women	0.0	0.0	0.0	0.0	6.7	0.0	2.8
No answer							
Men	2.9	10.0	10.6	11.7	15.4	*	*
Women	1.7	6.0	10.4	12.2	21.9	15.9	22.0

*Only women members were included in the study.

Note: Total N = 1,517.

TABLE 3.4

Marital Status of Respondents
(in percents)

Marital Status	Postal	Meat Cutters	Electrical	Custodial	Store	Hospital	Garment
Married							
Men	81.0	76.6	80.2	71.3	55.1	*	*
Women	39.3	42.9	63.2	40.8	51.8	55.0	46.7
Divorced, widowed, separated							
Men	6.6	8.5	5.0	8.8	5.1	*	*
Women	41.1	30.6	24.2	48.0	27.7	25.0	28.9
Single							
Men	12.4	14.9	14.9	19.9	39.7	*	*
Women	19.6	26.5	12.6	11.2	20.5	20.0	24.4
No answer							
Men	1.4	6.0	2.9	0.7	0.0	*	*
Women	3.4	2.0	1.0	0.0	1.8	4.8	1.1

*Only women members were included in the study.

Note: Total N = 1,517.

percent for Custodial Assistants'. Far fewer working men are in this category; questionnaire responses show a low of 5 percent among Electrical Union men and a high of only 8.8 percent among male custodial assistants.

The difference in proportions of men and women who are single is less in each of the unions except the Store Workers' Union, where 39.7 percent of the men report they are single compared to 20.5 percent of the women. The highest percentage of single women is in the Meat Cutters' Union, where we have already noted the large number of part-time workers who are young students.

More men than women report they are married in each of the unions. The lowest percentage is among Store Worker men, but even that is 55.1 percent, and the highest is among Postal men, where 81 percent are married. In no union, however, are more than two-thirds of the women married, and in four of the seven unions less than one-half the women are married. Again this underscores the economic reasons that bring increasing numbers of women into the work force.

The proportion in the national labor force of single women combined with those widowed, divorced, or separated, according to data published by the Bureau of Labor Statistics, is 42 percent. This compares with our study, if we combine the two groups for the women in each union, as follows:

Responding Women Unionists, Single, Widowed,
Divorced, Separated (combined figures)

	Percent
Electrical	36.8
Hospital	45.0
Store workers	48.2
Garment	53.3
Meat cutters	57.1
Custodial	59.2
Postal	60.7

Table 3.5 displays the proportions of men and women who are the sole support of their families. The number of women who are the sole support of households ranges from a low of 43.4 percent among store workers to a high of 62.1 percent among custodial assistants. This does not differ markedly from the population in general, where more than one-half of the women heads of families work outside the home. It does underscore again how many women work primarily because of economic need.

TABLE 3.5

Sole Support of Families
(in percents)

	Sole Support		Not Sole Support		No Answer	
	Men	Women	Men	Women	Men	Women
Postal	64.5	53.4	35.5	46.6	0.7	0.0
Meat Cutters	79.2	42.9	20.8	57.1	4.0	2.0
Electrical	67.0	45.2	33.0	54.8	3.8	3.1
Custodial	75.6	62.1	24.4	37.9	1.5	3.1
Store	65.4	43.4	34.6	56.6	0.0	7.0
Hospital	*	60.3	*	39.7	*	7.9
Garment	*	50.6	*	49.4	*	11.0

*Only women were included in the study.

Note: Total N = 1,517.

The numbers and ages of respondents' children are
shown in Tables 3.6 and 3.7. The large percentage of
women in the Meat Cutters' Union that have no children
probably reflects the younger part-time workers. The
custodial assistants are the most likely to have five or
six children; more than twice as many do than is reported
by the next largest group, IUE women. They are also the
group most likely to have even larger families.

In four of the unions, a majority of the women respondents have children over the age of 18. However, in
two unions, Postal and Hospital, a third or more women
have school-aged children. It is in the Postal Union that
we find as many as 20 percent of the women have children
under age six. It is no surprise, therefore, that this is
the union with the most interest in and pressure for child
care.

The work histories of men and women respondents are
presented in Table 3.8. More than half of all the women
in each union studied have always worked. The range is
from a low of 55 percent among store workers to a high of
75.6 percent among garment women. The pattern of blue-
collar women, at least in an urban environment, cannot be
said to be one of leaving work for a period of time while
children are young, and later returning. The proportion
of women indicating they had done this ranged from a low

TABLE 3.6

Numbers of Children of Respondents
(in percents)

Numbers of Children	Postal	Meat Cutters	Electrical	Custodial	Store	Hospital	Garment
None							
Men	14.0	17.4	14.6	20.7	49.3	*	*
Women	19.3	39.6	22.1	21.6	32.0	24.2	31.5
One child							
Men	23.3	15.2	14.6	14.9	14.7	*	*
Women	26.3	12.5	26.7	22.7	19.4	22.6	26.0
2 to 4 children							
Men	57.4	63.0	66.7	52.1	33.3	*	*
Women	49.1	41.7	44.2	37.5	45.6	48.4	39.7
5 to 6 children							
Men	5.4	4.3	3.1	9.9	2.7	*	*
Women	5.3	6.3	7.0	14.8	2.9	3.2	2.7
More than 6							
Men	0.0	0.0	1.0	2.5	0.0	*	*
Women	0.0	0.0	0.0	3.4	0.0	1.6	0.0
No answer							
Men	7.2	8.0	7.7	11.7	3.8	*	*
Women	1.7	4.0	10.4	10.2	9.6	1.6	19.8

*Only women were included in the study.

Note: Total N = 1,517.

71

TABLE 3.7

Ages of Children of Respondents
(in percents)

Ages of Children	Postal	Meat Cutters	Electrical	Custodial	Store	Hospital	Garment
Infant to 18 years							
Men	11.8	8.1	7.6	17.3	7.9	*	*
Women	6.5	13.3	0.0	1.5	3.0	15.9	4.2
Under 6 years only							
Men	10.0	13.5	13.9	9.2	15.8	*	*
Women	19.6	3.3	3.0	4.5	4.5	11.4	2.1
6 to 18 years only							
Men	23.6	29.7	22.8	28.6	28.9	*	*
Women	39.1	26.7	22.7	12.1	10.4	40.9	18.8
Over 18 years only							
Men	32.7	35.1	40.1	25.5	36.8	*	*
Women	30.4	43.3	51.5	51.5	68.7	18.2	68.8
Below 18 and over 18							
Men	21.8	13.5	15.2	19.4	10.5	*	*
Women	4.3	13.3	22.7	30.3	13.4	13.6	6.3
No answer (includes no children)							
Men	20.9	26.0	24.0	28.5	51.3	*	*
Women	20.7	40.0	31.3	32.7	41.2	30.2	47.3

*Only women were included in the study.

Note: Total N = 1,517.

TABLE 3.8

Work History of Men and Women in Seven Study Unions

(in percents)

Work History	Postal	Meat Cutters	Electrical	Custodial	Store	Hospital	Garment
Just begun to work							
Men	0.7	2.0	2.0	1.5	2.6	*	*
Women	1.8	6.3	2.2	3.2	5.4	0.0	5.8
Stopped for children, returned							
Men	0.7	2.0	0.0	0.0	0.0	*	*
Women	33.3	25.0	23.7	13.8	25.2	11.7	16.3
Stopped, other reasons, returned							
Men	2.9	4.1	1.0	4.4	5.2	*	*
Women	3.5	12.5	10.8	12.8	9.9	13.3	2.3
Always worked							
Men	95.0	91.8	97.1	93.3	92.2	*	*
Women	61.4	56.3	54.8	70.2	55.0	75.0	75.6
Other							
Men	0.7	0.0	0.0	0.7	0.0	*	*
Women	0.0	0.0	8.6	0.0	4.5	0.0	0.0
No answer							
Men	0.0	2.0	1.9	1.5	2.6	*	*
Women	1.7	4.0	3.1	4.1	1.5	4.8	5.5

*Only women were included in the study.

Note: Total N = 1,517.

73

of 11.7 percent among hospital workers to a high of 33.3 percent among postal workers; six of the seven unions show that a quarter or less of the women members have followed this pattern.

Table 3.9 shows skill level and skill differences between men and women in each union. As noted earlier, these are sharp except among postal workers, who work at the same skill level (most are semiskilled), and custodial assistants, who are overwhelmingly unskilled. Of the unions that include a substantial number of skilled jobs in their jurisdictions, three had both men and women respondents. Here the proportion of male skilled workers ranged from 38 to 100 percent, while among women respondents, it went from 0.0 percent to a high of only 16 percent holding skilled positions.

Table 3.10 indicates levels of job satisfaction of respondents. More women than men seem to "enjoy" their jobs, though the differences are not great. The percentage of workers who "dislike" their jobs is similar also. The divergence between the attitudes of men and women appears more clearly in the middle categories. Among meat cutters, for example, far more women than men are "slightly dissatisfied" (30 percent compared to 14 percent); over half the men in that union say they are satisfied, and only 38 percent of the women.

The women indicating most satisfaction with their jobs are in those industries where there is direct contact with the person served (hospital, store) or where the worker often performs the entire operation herself (dressmakers). In each of the seven unions, a majority of the women indicate they are satisfied or feel even better about their jobs, but the percentage jumps significantly in the three unions mentioned above.

Union (women only)	"Satisfied or Better" with Job (percent)
Custodial	57
Postal	57
Meat cutters	60
Electrical	67
Hospital	71
Dressmakers	73
Store	85

The highest dissatisfaction is found among men and women postal workers, women meat cutters, women custodial assistants, and men in the electrical industry (followed

TABLE 3.9

Job Skill
(in percents)

Level of Skill as Reported by Respondents	Postal	Meat Cutters	Electrical	Custodial	Store	Hospital	Garment
Skilled							
Men	2.3	89.6	66.3	3.9	37.9	*	*
Women	3.7	0.0	16.3	4.5	5.7	0.0	90.2
Semiskilled							
Men	84.5	8.3	22.1	1.6	50.0	*	*
Women	85.2	36.7	66.3	1.1	90.6	31.4	4.9
Unskilled							
Men	13.2	2.1	11.6	94.5	12.1	*	*
Women	11.1	63.3	17.4	94.3	3.8	68.6	4.9
No answer							
Men	7.2	4.0	8.7	7.3	15.4	*	*
Women	6.9	2.0	10.4	10.2	7.0	19.0	9.9

*Only women members were included in the study.

Note: Total N = 1,517.

TABLE 3.10

Job Satisfaction of Respondents
(in percents)

Job Satisfaction	Postal	Meat Cutters	Electrical	Custodial	Store	Hospital	Garment
Dislike job							
Men	13.0	8.2	11.9	7.7	5.3	*	*
Women	13.0	8.0	1.1	9.4	3.6	0.0	4.5
Slightly dissatisfied							
Men	34.1	14.3	34.7	28.5	22.7	*	*
Women	29.6	30.0	31.9	32.3	19.8	29.0	22.7
Satisfied							
Men	35.5	51.0	34.7	39.2	34.7	*	*
Women	38.9	38.0	50.0	37.5	36.9	37.1	36.4
Well satisfied							
Men	6.5	8.2	8.9	14.6	10.7	*	*
Women	9.3	6.0	4.3	7.3	8.1	21.0	15.9
Enjoy job							
Men	10.9	18.4	9.9	10.0	26.7	*	*
Women	9.3	18.0	12.8	13.5	31.5	12.9	20.5
No answer							
Men	0.7	2.0	2.9	5.1	3.8	*	*
Women	6.9	0.0	2.1	2.0	2.6	1.6	3.3

*Only women members were included in the study.

closely by the women there). In discussing these findings with leaders in the respective unions, various explanations emerged.

1. Postal: Men and women do much the same work, and both respond negatively to the noise and pace of the machines and to the impersonal and bureaucratic structure of the post office. There is little mobility for individuals in this industry, and their education level is relatively high. However, job security and the possibility of early retirement compensate in some measure.

2. Meat wrappers and checkers: Women in the Meat Cutters' Union are indicating their response to dead-end, low-skill jobs with no chance for advancement.

3. Custodial assistants: Almost half of the women in this group are somewhat dissatisfied or dislike their jobs. The union's leaders believe that this reflects, in part, the loneliness of their work and, in part, the fact that many of them work 30 hours and feel that, because of the job freeze in effect at the time of the study, they are expected to compensate for the short-handedness by working harder.

4. Electrical workers: This group shares many of the problems that postal workers have in working conditions, machines whose pace they cannot control, and the fact that they do a small piece of the total production work with little or no contact with the finished product or the consumer. Many of the less skilled are on assembly lines, and more than one in four are on piece work.

Leaders of the Garment Union believe that the figure on job dissatisfaction (27.2 percent) for Local 22 members does not reflect dissatisfaction with the kind of work the member does, but with the particular shop she may be in, the supervisor or boss she has, or with a certain style or fabric on which she may have been working at the time of the study. The union feels strongly that the women really like their work.

Table 3.11 shows the length of time respondents have been members of their unions. In the case of hospital workers and custodial assistants, the figures reflect the fact that the unions themselves are young, and most members have come in only within the last 10 years. In the eldest of the unions, Local 22 of the garment workers, more than three out of four members have belonged for more than 10 years.

The influx of women into the Postal Union since Executive Order 10988 is indicated by the figures of that union, which show that 89.1 percent of the women members have joined only since 1962.

The final table in this chapter, Table 3.12, indicates the advancement opportunities that respondents see for themselves. This question was not included on the questionnaire distributed to the Meat Cutters' Union.

Among custodial assistants, where there is little actual chance for advancement, the percentage of men and women who believe they can advance is quite high. Union leaders consider the response is due to emphasis in union publications on DC 37's training and education program. Custodial assistants can qualify for jobs that would move them out of their division (blue collar) into a clerical line if they study and pass the civil service tests. A number of custodial women, indeed, have joined the typing classes offered through the union and also the high school equivalency programs. Men appear more convinced than women that they can advance, and it is true that only they were qualified formerly to take the examinations for superintendent. These are now open to both men and women. The union currently is working to create new lines for promotion, and that may account for some of the optimism among Local 1547 members. In addition, many of the 30-hour employees (women) are looking forward to becoming 40-hour employees and receiving larger paychecks. Technically not a promotion, it is, however, an improvement which they know the union is seeking on their behalf.

The high number of hospital workers who believe they can advance reflects a reality. The union's training program, which offers opportunities for almost all who wish to move up the job ladder through study, has been the means for advancement achieved.

The high proportion of Local 22, dressmakers, who believe they can advance may seem hard to explain, since the vast majority are already skilled operators who will remain at their same jobs indefinitely. It is probable that these workers interpret "advancement" to mean an increase in rate of pay, since training for more skilled positions is not part of the experience of women in this union.

Many women seem unsure about their advancement possibilities; in most unions there are substantially more "unsure" women than men. This is not surprising when we recall that women generally hold the lower-skilled jobs-- and have had little opportunities for moving out of them. The high proportion of postal workers, men and women, who

Length of Time in Union of Respondents
(in percents)

Years in Union	Postal	Meat Cutters	Electrical	Custodial	Store	Hospital	Garment
Less than 2							
Men	2.3	12.5	13.3	15.4	17.8	*	*
Women	3.6	14.0	6.9	12.1	13.5	9.3	3.6
2 to 10 years							
Men	45.9	29.2	60.2	73.1	42.5	*	*
Women	85.5	46.0	47.1	78.0	37.8	81.5	17.9
More than 10							
Men	51.9	58.3	26.5	11.5	39.7	*	*
Women	10.9	40.0	46.0	9.9	48.6	9.3	78.6
No answer							
Men	4.3	4.0	5.8	5.1	6.4	*	*
Women	5.2	0.0	9.4	7.1	2.6	14.3	7.7

*Only women members were included in the study.

Note: N = 1,517.

TABLE 3.12

Advancement Possibilities--Respondent Estimate
(in percents)

	Postal	Meat Cutters[a]	Electrical	Custodial	Store	Hospital	Garment
Yes							
Men	58.2		53.7	56.8	46.6	b	b
Women	56.6		27.5	49.5	30.0	57.1	47.4
No							
Men	29.1		24.2	14.4	26.0	b	b
Women	18.9		38.5	23.2	36.0	19.6	38.5
Not sure							
Men	12.7		22.1	28.8	27.4	b	b
Women	24.5		34.1	27.4	34.0	23.2	14.1
No answer							
Men	3.6		8.7	3.6	6.4	b	b
Women	8.6		5.2	3.1	12.3	11.1	14.3

[a] This question was not administered to Meat Cutters.
[b] Only women members were included in the study.

Note: Total N = 1,517.

think they can advance reflects the civil service nature of the job and, for women, the fact that seniority means an opportunity to bid off the night tour.

SUMMARY AND CONCLUSIONS

Each of the unions differs substantially from the others in the study in the kind of industry covered, size of union, length of time it had been organized, and in many cases, in its proportion of women members. The unions represent a spread of the major blue-collar and service occupations in New York City, and to this extent may be considered typical of local unions in this one urban center, though not, of course, for the country as a whole.

Our reception in each union was friendly, open, and cooperative, though initially and not surprisingly, leaders tended to be defensive. The subject area is a touchy one, particularly since the top leader in each union is a man. However, no researcher could have asked for more assistance than we received from those unions, who in different ways enlisted the help of staff, officers, and rank and file leaders and members wherever and whenever it was needed. This was particularly important in terms of getting the questionnaires into the hands of the widest possible number of rank and file members, which enabled our returns to reflect accurately the membership composition of each union. These questionnaire returns were of great interest to the union leadership, for whom it provided new information in some areas and confirmed their knowledge or hunches in others.

In comparing findings for the seven unions, we found that the age of the women members in a majority of the unions tends to be over 45, somewhat higher than the national average for employed women (39 years). This relates to the data indicating that, in all but two of the unions, women exceed the national average in the percent with only some high school education or less, since the younger the worker's age, the more likely he or she is to have completed high school. Postal worker women and storeworkers, with fewer women members in that educational category than the national norm, reflect the postal service job requirements on the one hand and the white-collar nature of retail store work on the other.

Looking at the educational data another way, more men in four of the five unions with male respondents have

completed high school than the national norm for male workers while this holds true for but two of the seven unions
in terms of their women members. It underscores the fact
that when union women indicate they want "education" to
help them become more active in their unions, a point which
will be discussed in succeeding chapters, they know what
they are talking about. Indeed, they do show up in the
data as having less education than the men, and this may
well contribute to their sense of inadequacy and to feelings that they are not held in the same respect in which
they hold the male members of the unions. In the two
unions that stand out as exceptions to this, we find that
postal men and women have substantially the same educational levels, again reflecting civil service job requirements, while figures for meatcutter women are skewed by
the number of young students, mostly women, who compose
the part-time work force and make up 50 percent of the
union's women members.

Marital status and sole support figures, no surprise
to the union's leadership, reinforce what is known about
the economic reasons bringing so many women into the labor
force. In all but one union the percent of women widowed,
divorced, or separated exceeded the national average for
employed women, running as high as 61 percent in one of
the unions.

Study data on the ages of children may prove especially useful for assessing child care needs--or lack of such
needs--when drawing up collective bargaining demands.
Only two unions show any high percent of women with children under age 18, but in those two, fully a third or more
of the women have children of school age or younger. In
the postal union, women are now interested in pressing for
incorporating child care as a demand, and the data indicate 20 percent of the women have children under age six.

The usual assumptions that women interrupt their work
lives to raise a family do not hold true for most of the
women in this study. Here we find that a high percent
have not interrupted their work lives to any great degree
for children. The largest numbers who did take time off
for child-rearing are found in the two unions with women
having the highest educational levels, postal and storeworkers, where more than three-quarters have a high school
degree or better. Clearly most of the women in these New
York City locals have had to work for a living most of
their adult lives, and our data do not differ from widely
prevalent statistics relating education, skill and income
levels.

81

The wide gap in skill levels of jobs held by men and by women in the unions studied, except for those jobs covered by civil service, is not unlike figures emerging across the country, where today it is becoming necessary to seek remedies to this situation. Union upgrading, training and other programs, as well as collective bargaining agreements, point to increasing sensitivity to this need. So do pressures exerted by government equal employment agencies, and changes being instituted by employers. The outlook is bright for women workers, though at times progress seems slow indeed.

Studies of job satisfaction, so prevalent today, rarely include women workers. Study data we pulled from the seven union comparisons indicate that women, too, tend to be dissatisfied with dead end jobs that are dull and routine. Women who have contact with other people during their working day, who feel they are of service to others, and who have some control over the rate of their work or in planning how to accomplish that work, show a higher level of job satisfaction. However, the women in these seven unions, by and large, are less sure that they can advance on the job than are the men, and this reflects reality, since they tend to hold those jobs offering least advancement.

In Chapter 4 we move from the job area to focus on what union men and women regard as barriers to active participation in their unions, continuing to utilize statistical data from the questionnaire returns. Chapter 5 turns from these data to the union leaders and rank and file activists themselves, who speak through interviews that were conducted by the authors and by rank and file women leaders from each of the participating unions.

NOTES

1. Arthur Summerfield, U.S. Mail (New York: Holt, Rinehart & Winston, 1960), pp. 49, 50.
2. Ibid., pp. 48-49.
3. Matthew Bowyer, They Carried the Mail (Washington, D.C.: Robert Luce Inc., 1972), pp. 78, 80.
4. For this and certain other material about Local 342, we are indebted to Austin Perlow's We Found Out We Had a Union to Go To, published by Local 342 in 1968, pages unnumbered.

5. Laurie Taub, "Should Women Be Meat Cutters?" a project of the Metropolitan Office, Cornell University, New York State School of Industrial and Labor Relations, January 1972, p. 12.

6. See also Al Nash's article, "Hospital Values, Conflicts and Supervisory Practice," Personnel Journal (December 1973): 1060. Nash finds in his study of blue-collar workers at Montefiore Hospital, also members of District 1199, that these workers have a high level of job satisfaction attributable to the freedom of control over their pace of work, job security, good pay, and working conditions compared with those they previously experienced (many came from Puerto Rico, Haiti, Cuba, and other Latin American or West Indian countries). Patient contact gives them a greater interest in their jobs and a feeling of the importance of their work.

7. The New York Times, February 19, 1973, p. 25.

Despite differences in industry and occupation, in
size of union, and personal characteristics of union members, certain statements can be made common to the union
men and women of this study. The women tend to be older
than the men, less likely to have completed high school
but also more likely to have education beyond high school.
They tend to hold less-skilled jobs, and a high proportion
is unmarried or no longer living with their husbands.
Among the seven unions, an average of 7 percent of the
women had children under the age of six; nationally, however, more than one out of three working mothers have
children under six. The proportion of women who were the
sole support of their households ranged from 43 to 62 percent. In every union surveyed, the majority of the women
have always worked; they have not interrupted their work
lives to care for young children nor for other reasons.
    Having learned something about the lives of the women
in the study and about their unions and their jobs, we
turn in this chapter to an examination of the way their
circumstances affect their willingness to undertake union
activity. The opinions of union leaders on this question,
reported in Chapter 2, generally indicate that they find
women difficult to involve in union work; they feel women's
obligations require them to be at home when union meetings
are going on; they believe women tend to be afraid of increased union responsibility; they find women sell themselves short.
    What do the women themselves have to say? Do their
views correspond to those of union leaders? Of rank and
file men? How do women view their own involvement in
union work?

UNION PARTICIPATION

Most respondents have engaged only in such broad activities as attending union meetings, using the grievance
procedure, or voting in union elections. Others, however,
have gone on to an active role in shaping union policy.
They have served on committees, been shop stewards, or
held union office.

In order to distinguish between the attitudes of members who have received union recognition and those who
have not, the replies of respondents have been matched to
their general activity level. The responses of those who
have had an active role are broken out from those who,
though their interest in the union may be high, have not
held union positions. The distinction is especially important to draw in this study since the distribution of
questionnaires varied among the different unions.

As in Chapter 2, which considered the responses to an
overview survey of certain New York City local unions, we
remind the reader that those who return questionnaires
are more likely than others to have an interest in the
subject: in this case, their union. Thus, the proportion
of respondents who have taken an active part in union affairs is probably higher than would be expected in the
union as a whole.

Table 4.1 compares the proportion of respondents who
have not held union positions with those who have in the
seven unions studied. In all cases, the men have had a
more active role than the women in shaping union policy,
usually considerably more. In the tables appearing in
this chapter, as in Chapter 3, the reader is reminded that
the unions are presented in the order of their proportion
of women members. The Postal Union has the lowest proportion of female membership, and Local 22 of the garment
workers has the highest.

Participation of Members without Union Position

It is apparent that in every union except the Meat
Cutters', women rank and filers are involved in more ways
than men without union positions. Women may not be as
visible, since they do not hold union positions as often
as men, but they are the backbone of the union in its day-
to-day affairs. They vote more, attend more meetings, go
to more educational and social events, and even file more
grievances [Table 4.2(A)].

TABLE 4.1

Level of Union Activity of Study Respondents
as Measured by Union Positions Held
(in percents)

	Unionists with Low Levels of Activity		Active Unionists		No Answer	
	Men	Women	Men	Women	Men	Women
Postal	33.1	75.0	66.9	25.0	2.2	3.4
Meat cutters	59.1	54.3	40.9	45.7	12.0	30.0
Electrical	52.6	80.6	47.4	19.4	8.7	3.1
Custodial	80.4	81.0	19.6	19.0	18.2	19.4
Store	49.3	65.5	50.7	34.5	6.4	3.5
Hospital*	--	90.2	--	9.8	--	3.2
Garment*	--	47.2	--	52.8	--	2.2

*Only women members were included in the study.

The respondents of two unions report a considerably higher use of the grievance procedure than do the others: the Electrical Workers' (IUE) and the Postal Union. The explanation lies in the character of the work the men and women perform, particularly the women. Most IUE women are on assembly line piece work involving considerable stress. The line moves inexorably; the foreman tends to oversee the work closely and is himself under pressure for high productivity; the work is monotonous and the breaks from it are welcome. In such an atmosphere, grievances are likely to burgeon. Postal work shares some of the same qualities. Surveillance in the postal system is omnipresent, a fact that bothers workers and makes them as quick to take umbrage as the supervisor is quick to find fault. Women are often assigned to the mail-sorting machine, a lonely job and one that is both noisy and dusty.
Members show unusually high participation in the education programs of three Locals: the Custodial Assistants', Meat Cutters', and Hospital Workers'.
The Custodial Assistants' Local, as an affiliate of District Council 37, AFSCME, shares in the education programming of that union. DC 37's education efforts rank high among union priorities, and its members, as civil servants, know their job advancement lies in successfully passing civil service examinations. Custodial assistants

TABLE 4.2(A)

Participation in Union Affairs of Rank and File Members without Union Position
(in percents)

	Postal	Meat Cutters	Electrical	Custodial	Store	Hospital*	Garment*
Used the grievance procedure							
Men	10.3	0.0	22.1	10.7	6.8	--	--
Women	17.9	2.9	32.3	11.4	8.2	4.9	3.4
Attended a membership meeting							
Men	19.9	54.5	38.9	73.2	46.6	--	--
Women	41.1	45.7	72.0	74.7	60.0	80.3	44.9
Attended a union social event							
Men	8.8	15.9	4.2	11.6	6.8	--	--
Women	28.6	2.9	11.8	22.8	15.5	37.7	22.5
Attended a union education program							
Men	0.0	13.6	2.1	11.6	2.7	--	--
Women	3.6	11.4	4.3	22.8	1.8	11.5	9.0
Voted in a union election							
Men	31.6	43.2	48.4	16.1	42.5	--	--
Women	69.6	28.6	73.1	16.5	60.9	88.5	38.2

*Only women members were included in the study.

are exposed to the union newspaper's exhortations and are, correspondingly, education conscious. Among this union's respondents, women are almost twice as likely as men to have taken some course offered by the union. The director of DC 37's Blue-Collar Division at the time of the study speculated that the reason for women's higher interest was that, as minority group members, they are especially conscious of upward mobility for their children and view education as a major route to it. After urging their children to take education seriously, it is natural that, when the opportunity is available to them through the union, the women would reach out to take advantage of it for themselves. On the other hand, many male custodians hold two jobs and find it more difficult to attend classes or to participate actively in the union.

The Meat Cutters' Local 342 is another union that attaches high value to education. As was noted in the preceding chapter, the reform administration of this Local has used education to revitalize the once-moribund union. Education is seen also as a means of offering other opportunities to women members whose jobs provide no articulated advancement.

Hospital Workers' District 1199 conducts its own training and upgrading program, which is important to the career advancement of its predominantly female membership. In addition, the union conducts a series of patient care conferences for all its members.

The data on the participation of members in union activities are presented in two tables. Table 4.2(A) relates the union activity of men and women who have never been committee members or shop stewards, nor run for or held a union office. Responses of members who have sought or received union positions and the proportions of members who did not respond to the question are found in Table 4.2(B).

Participation of Members Who Sought
or Held Union Positions

The higher the union position, the fewer women are found to hold it. Women are most likely to have been shop stewards or committee members. A lower proportion is chairmen of committees, has run for office, or served as elected officers. In all categories measured, however, women tend to have been less active participants than men.

TABLE 4.2(B)

Participation in Union Affairs of Members Who Sought or Held Union Position
(in percents)

	Postal	Meat Cutters	Electrical	Custodial	Store	Hospital*	Garment*
Been a committee member							
Men	22.8	18.2	35.8	5.4	31.5	--	--
Women	7.1	34.3	15.1	8.9	21.8	3.3	21.3
Been a shop steward, delegate, or shop chairman							
Men	65.4	34.1	43.2	15.2	47.9	--	--
Women	25.0	25.7	16.1	16.5	30.0	8.2	43.8
Been chairman of a committee							
Men	15.4	9.1	13.7	2.7	9.6	--	--
Women	1.8	8.6	2.2	2.5	7.3	1.6	12.4
Run for a union officer							
Men	30.1	11.4	20.0	5.4	9.6	--	--
Women	3.6	8.6	3.2	6.3	3.6	1.6	9.0
Been elected to an office							
Men	30.1	6.8	18.9	4.5	9.6	--	--
Women	7.1	5.7	4.3	3.8	4.5	0.0	10.1
No answer [Tables 4.2(A) and 4.2(B)]							
Men	2.2	12.0	8.7	18.2	6.4	--	--
Women	3.4	30.0	3.1	19.4	3.5	3.2	2.2

*Only women members were included in the study.

The custodial assistants' pattern differs from that of the other unions. In that Local the only place where women's involvement does not equal or exceed that of men's is in the number who have been elected to office. For example, more women have run for office than have been elected, but for men, about the same proportion who run seem to get elected.

In the Meat Cutters' Union, the high proportion of women committee members represents a skew in the population that returned questionnaires. The Meat Cutters' have an organized Women's Division whose interest in union participation is high. Responses from members of this group exceed their proportions in the union.

Although women hospital workers record the highest level of activity among union members holding no committee or other union position, their percentage in union posts is unusually small. One reason is that the members of this Local are the youngest of all in the survey (the largest number is between age 25 and 35). In addition, 60 percent report they are the sole support of their households and, as will be seen later, home responsibilities are considered by hospital workers to be a major limit on their union activity. The fact that District 1199 is a young union and the hospital in which the survey was conducted has had a union contract only since 1964 may contribute to the low representation of those workers in union posts.

Table 4.2(B) characterizes the activity of the men and women who have sought or held union positions in the seven unions surveyed.

PERSONAL AND SOCIOCULTURAL REASONS FOR LOW PARTICIPATION

All members were asked what they regarded as the major barriers to their becoming more involved in union affairs. The questions were grouped around barriers that are personal to each member, those that are related to the job, and those related to the union. A comparison of the responses for men and women shows that although in large measure they agree on many things, the priorities assigned are often different.

Responses grouped as personal or sociocultural reasons affecting participation were given in answer to the question: What would have to change in your life to make it easier for you to participate in union affairs?

The largest number selected fewer home responsibilities, or needing more information about the union. Men ranked information higher; women, home responsibilities.

Next in importance for both men and women was either the need to feel more competent before they undertake active union roles, or the desire to go to meetings with someone. Men tend to rate competency higher, while women wish someone to accompany them to meetings. The women's priority is considered a reflection of their fear of late night hours rather than an indication of any feelings of greater competency.

Both men and women consider that knowing more people who would be at the meetings would be a significant inducement to greater union activity, but women were less likely to think so. Women were also less likely to see union activity as requiring them to drop activities in other groups they like.

The need to speak better English is felt acutely by women in the Garment Union who consider it their greatest barrier to further participation in the union. The large number of Hispanic-American members (estimates run as high as 50 percent) explains the response, and for them, the union offers language classes. But other unionists feel this need as well, particularly hospital workers and custodial assistants.

There are in every union some women who think men are better at union affairs. The proportions are so similar that we conclude that at this time about 1 woman out of 10 is likely to hold the opinion. Until she sees other women coping successfully with union office, or until she has more confidence in her own abilities, that woman probably will not be available for union work. In the Meat Cutters' Union, however, 2 women out of 10 agree with the statement, "I am a woman and think men are better at union affairs." A clue to their attitude may lie in the fact that fully 8 percent of the male respondents in the union took the trouble to cross out the word "woman" in the statement and to check the revised version, "I am a man and think men are better at union affairs."

Women do not see themselves as lacking interest in their union. More men than women in four of the five unions that surveyed men checked: "Just not interested in union affairs." In the only case where not one single respondent checked this choice, it was the women of the Custodial Assistants' Union that so responded. Yet many union leaders see women as less interested. The explanation may be that leaders expect "interested" members to take active roles in the union, whereas women consider that although their interest and goodwill are as high or higher than men's, interest alone cannot free them for what they would like to do.

Evidence of the special limits on women is found not only in their greater home responsibilities and vulnerability to unsafe night streets, but also in their response to the choice: "My husband or wife would have to agree to my being more active in the union." Women were more likely than men to check this response. From interviews with rank and file women, reported in Chapter 5, it is clear that their husband's attitudes are indeed an important factor.

Strikingly clear, however, is the fact that women are available for greater participation. The proportions of women in every union except the Meat Cutters' that responded that nothing needs change is so similar that we conclude that there are no personal reasons limiting the union activity of almost 2 women out of 10. These are the women who appear to be sufficiently free of home responsibilities, who have enough confidence in themselves, enough union information, and enough interest in the union to be willing to give more time to it. In two unions, the Electrical and the Store Workers', "Nothing would have to change," was the second ranking response of women members. Although many of these women are union activists, sizable proportions are not [Tables 4.3(B) and 4.3(C)].

Nevertheless, women are more likely than men to report personal reasons for limiting their activity. In every union except the Custodial Assistants' Local, more men than women consider that nothing needs change. Indeed, it is the first response for the men of three Locals, Postal, Electrical, and Store Workers', and is another indication of the greater flexibility men often have in the way they spend their nonworking hours.

A special note is required for the response of members of the Meat Cutters', 98 percent of whom believe that something would have to change in order for them to become more active. The same major reasons are cited by meat cutters as are cited by members of other unions for restricting their union activity, but male meat cutters differ dramatically in their assent to two other statements: "Would want to go to meetings with someone," and "Fewer activities in other groups I like." The first response is a comment on the wide geographic area covered by Local 342. The union has had difficulty in finding conveniently located meeting halls. There are transportation problems in Long Island and Staten Island, and personal cars or car pools are necessary to get around. Union officials interpreting the second response suggest that many members are involved in community activities or in home ownership responsibilities. The large number of part-time students who belong to this union also contributes to that response.

In summary, women appear more interested than men in union affairs, and 2 out of 10 see no personal barrier to increasing their participation. Women and men both express a keen desire for more information about the union and for greater competency before they consider themselves qualified for larger leadership responsibilities. Women are more tied down by home responsibilities, by the attitudes of their spouses toward union activity, and by the absence of someone with whom they could go to meetings. Men appear more interested in knowing people who will be at the meetings, and more likely to be engaged in other-than-union activities they might have to drop if they were to give more time to the union. Roughly 1 woman in 10 thinks men are better at union matters. Table 4.3(A) describes respondents' views of the personal factors that limit union activity.

Union Activists Compared with Rank and File Members

Since it will be useful to understand which personal barriers are most important to less active members, and which are important to those already active, the responses of each group are reported separately in Tables 4.3(B) and 4.3(C).

Members without any union post are far more likely than others to cite personal factors that affect their union participation. Home responsibilities loom large for women who are interested in the union but not active in an official capacity. In other respects, their needs are the same as those of women who are actively engaged in union affairs, but they tend to give them less weight.

Perhaps the most striking finding is that in three areas of special importance to both men and women, the needs expressed by men who are not actively involved in the union are those cited by women who are union activists. The desire for more information about the union is higher among "less active" men in the majority of unions that surveyed men but among "active" women in four of the seven that included women, although usually in lower proportions.

TABLE 4.3(A)

Personal Factors That Limit Union Activity
(in percents)

	Postal	Meat Cutters	Electrical	Custodial	Store	Hospital*	Garme
Nothing would have changed in my personal life							
Men	40.9	2.5	37.3	11.9	26.6	--	--
Women	16.1	2.1	20.2	15.7	15.2	14.5	17.
Fewer home responsibilities							
Men	18.9	25.0	24.5	20.7	20.3	--	--
Women	32.1	35.4	34.5	25.8	42.9	43.6	22.
More information about union							
Men	28.3	32.5	19.6	52.6	18.8	--	--
Women	33.9	31.3	21.4	33.7	10.5	34.5	17.
Fewer activities in other groups I like							
Men	8.7	17.5	11.8	10.4	9.4	--	--
Women	3.6	4.2	6.0	7.9	11.4	10.9	6.
Need to speak better English							
Men	3.9	12.5	5.9	22.2	4.7	--	--
Women	1.8	4.2	11.9	14.6	5.7	18.2	32.
Need to feel more competent							
Men	7.1	22.5	12.7	24.4	6.3	--	--
Women	17.9	8.3	11.9	25.8	7.6	14.5	17.
Would want to go to meetings with someone							
Men	5.5	22.5	2.9	16.3	9.4	--	--
Women	14.3	22.9	16.7	22.5	14.3	12.7	22.
Would want to know more people who would be at the meetings							
Men	12.6	15.0	7.8	28.1	14.1	--	--
Women	16.1	12.5	9.5	20.2	8.6	9.1	19.
My husband or wife would have to agree to my being active in the union							
Men	3.9	20.0	4.9	5.9	3.1	--	--
Women	5.4	12.5	3.6	10.1	11.4	7.3	10.
I am a woman and think men are better at union affairs							
Men	0.0	7.5	1.0	0.0	1.6	--	--
Women	7.1	20.8	8.3	10.1	11.4	10.9	13.
I am just not interested in union affairs							
Men	1.6	10.0	9.8	4.4	6.3	--	--
Women	3.6	12.5	7.1	0.0	4.8	12.7	7.
No answer							
Men	8.6	1.5	1.9	1.5	17.9	--	--
Women	3.4	9.2	12.5	9.2	7.9	12.7	13.

*Only women members were included in the study.

Personal Barriers to Participation Most Frequently Cited by Members without Union Position (in percents)

	Postal	Meat Cutters	Electrical	Custodial	Store	Hospital*	Garment*
Nothing would have changed in my personal life							
Men	17.1	0.0	28.6	12.2	14.3	--	--
Women	14.3	0.0	15.2	16.4	7.5	14.3	12.8
Fewer home responsibilities							
Men	29.3	20.0	20.4	21.1	10.7	--	--
Women	38.1	27.8	42.4	23.0	47.8	46.9	17.9
More information about union							
Men	39.0	45.0	16.3	47.8	28.6	--	--
Women	31.0	33.3	24.2	31.1	10.4	30.6	12.8
Need to feel more competent							
Men	14.9	15.0	14.3	24.4	7.1	--	--
Women	19.0	0.0	12.1	26.2	6.0	12.2	23.1
Would want to go to meetings with someone							
Men	12.2	30.0	4.1	16.7	0.0	--	--
Women	7.1	27.8	12.1	19.7	13.4	10.2	25.6
Would want to know more people who would be at the meetings							
Men	9.8	15.0	6.1	25.6	10.7	--	--
Women	14.3	16.7	9.1	23.0	7.5	8.2	17.9
My husband or wife would have to agree to my being active in the union							
Men	2.4	30.0	4.1	4.4	0.0	--	--
Women	4.8	5.6	4.5	11.5	14.9	6.1	10.3
Fewer activities in other groups I like							
Men	12.2	20.0	18.4	4.4	14.3	--	--
Women	4.8	5.6	7.6	9.8	9.0	10.2	0.0

*Only women members were included in the study.

TABLE 4.3(C)

Personal Barriers Most Frequently Cited by Members Who Have Sought or Held Union Position
(in percents)

	Postal	Meat Cutters	Electrical	Custodial	Store	Hospital*	Garment*
Nothing would have changed in my personal life							
Men	51.8	7.1	50.0	13.6	36.4	--	--
Women	23.1	6.3	35.3	15.4	29.4	16.7	23.1
Fewer home responsibilities							
Men	14.1	35.7	29.5	31.8	27.3	--	--
Women	15.4	50.0	5.9	15.4	35.3	16.7	28.2
More information about union							
Men	23.5	14.3	18.2	63.6	9.1	--	--
Women	46.2	25.0	11.8	53.8	8.8	66.7	20.5
Need to feel more competent							
Men	8.2	28.6	9.1	22.7	6.1	--	--
Women	15.4	18.8	11.8	30.8	11.8	33.3	12.8
Would want to go to meetings with someone							
Men	2.4	21.4	2.3	18.2	18.2	--	--
Women	38.5	25.0	35.3	30.8	14.7	33.3	20.5
Would want to know more people who would be at the meetings							
Men	14.1	14.3	6.8	36.4	18.2	--	--
Women	23.1	6.3	11.8	15.4	11.8	16.7	20.5
My husband or wife would have to agree to my being active in the union							
Men	4.7	14.3	6.8	9.1	6.1	--	--
Women	7.7	18.8	0.0	7.7	5.9	16.7	10.3
Fewer activities in other groups I like							
Men	7.1	7.1	4.5	22.7	6.1	--	--
Women	0.0	6.3	0.0	0.0	17.6	16.7	12.8

*Only women members were included in the study.

96

The need for greater competence is even more identifiable with the responses of these two groups; in this case, women activists tend to cite it in higher proportions. The answer, "Would want to go to meetings with someone," shows the same pattern, although women generally consider it more important than men.

In interpreting this expression of the common needs of women activists and men who have not participated at the same level, we need to consider the context in which the responding women think of union activity. Women, even when active in the union, tend to hold lower union posts than those held by male activists. In most unions women have been in the same position during their years of participation, have become accustomed to the needs of that position, and have not thought much about moving to new, perhaps more demanding union posts. Many other women are relatively new to union work. But the winds of change are blowing, and they have been asked in this questionnaire, distributed by their union, to give thought to greater involvement. Their response is a serious expression of their feelings about the challenge. They believe they need to know more about union policy and to feel more competent before they can meet the challenge.

It is the active unionists among both men and women who want to know more people who will be at meetings, with men tending to value it more highly. Perhaps the sociability of union events is an important motivation for activists but less of a need for other members.

Men who hold union posts give a higher rank than other men or than women activists to "Fewer home responsibilities." They are also more likely than other men to check "My wife would have to agree to my being more active in the union." Taken together, these responses suggest that for this group, family obligations are a significant reason for not increasing their union participation. The agreement of their spouse, however, is more important to women, particularly to those who have not held official positions in the union.

There appears to be some support for the idea that activity in other groups competes with union work. Although other factors are given greater priority, the men who are less active in four of the five Locals that surveyed men are the ones responding that increased participation would mean "Fewer activities in other groups I like." This response is particularly characteristic of men as contrasted with women, regardless of their level of activity.

Table 4.3(B) reports the personal barriers cited most often by members without union position; Table 4.3(C) reports those cited by the activists.

JOB-RELATED REASONS AFFECTING UNION PARTICIPATION

Does a woman's work situation affect her participation in the union? The evidence of this study suggests that it does and that the job affects men differently. Women appear more apprehensive about confronting their supervisors, while men are more likely to think that union activity is worth doing if it provides them with upward job mobility.

The two responses reflecting these attitudes were the most important considerations for the men and women in every union. On the whole, women are less likely than men to relate any job factor to their union participation; both groups are less likely to rank job factors as important as those that are personal or union related.

Only in the Meat Cutters' was the response "Nothing about my job affects my union activity," given a low ranking. In that union, an unusually high proportion of men and women indicates that union activity would have to give them a better chance to get ahead on the job. Similarly, Meat Cutters' Union members attach considerably more importance than do other unionists to the choice: People who hold important jobs in the shop deserve union positions. Male meat cutters are more prone than any other group to indicate that supervisors are hard on active unionists, and they share with male custodial assistants the view that people who have been on the job longer should run the union.

Special note should also be made of the responses of the Postal Union. An indication of the similarity of viewpoint among men and women postal workers, a similarity which can be traced in many questionnaire replies, appears in their response to the question of whether job seniority should be a qualification for holding responsible union posts. In that union, where men have generally been employed far longer than women, only 5 percent of the men responded that long-time members should run the union. Furthermore, almost as many women as men think that members with important jobs deserve union positions, despite the fact that women are less likely to have those jobs. Their response contrasts with other unions where the men, who usually hold the better-paying jobs, are far more likely to agree with the statement and the women to disagree. The similarity of opinion may be related to the effect civil service has had on job tenure and advancement.

98

Union members tend to believe that seniority should play a role in determining union leadership. However, in three of the five unions that surveyed men, more men than women thought so.

Table 4.4(A) describes the job-related reasons for limited union activity.

Union Activists Compared with
Rank and File Members

Which union members cite job factors as of special concern? Generally, it is the members, particularly men, who are not involved in union affairs. In most unions, the men and women who have taken a role in shaping union policy are far more likely than others to agree with the choice, "Nothing about the job affects my union activity." Nevertheless, sizable proportions of activist members do have another opinion. The job factor ranked most important, "Supervisor should not make life hard for active unionists," is the opinion held by the activists in most unions. The responses ranked third and fourth, "People who hold important jobs in the shop deserve union positions" and "People who have been here longer should run the union," are chosen more often by those who have never sought or held a union position.

A member's level of participation in union matters seems to affect the opinions of women much more than it does men. For example, men who do not actively represent aggrieved workers in conflict with management appear to underestimate the difficulties and stress experienced by those who do. But among women the gap is far greater between the assessment of those who do not represent the workers and the concerns of those women who must: "Supervisor should not make life hard for active unionists."

| | Men | | Women | |
	Activists (percent)	Less Active (percent)	Activists (percent)	Less Active (percent)
Postal	33	28	54	27
Meat cutters	29	57	30	18
Electrical	32	29	25	19
Custodial	38	24	30	19
Store workers	11	11	29	12
Hospital*	--	--	40	25
Garment*	--	--	20	45

*Only women members were included in the study.

99

TABLE 4.4(A)

Job Factors That Affect Union Activity
(in percents)

	Postal	Meat Cutters	Electrical	Custodial	Store	Hospital*	Garment*
Supervisor should not make life hard for active unionists							
Men	31.6	40.0	28.9	26.8	10.5	--	--
Women	33.3	20.7	20.0	17.7	18.1	26.7	31.7
Union activity would have to give me a better chance to get ahead on the job							
Men	14.5	44.0	7.8	42.3	26.3	--	--
Women	13.7	27.6	12.0	22.8	6.9	22.2	21.7
I would need to work another shift							
Men	10.3	16.0	4.4	21.1	1.8	--	--
Women	11.8	0.0	1.3	11.4	0.0	6.7	0.0
I work part time and union doesn't affect me much							
Men	3.4	0.0	1.1	2.4	8.8	--	--
Women	0.0	20.7	0.0	10.1	5.6	0.0	0.0
People who hold important jobs in the shop deserve union position							
Men	4.3	32.0	10.0	15.4	12.3	--	--
Women	3.9	17.2	1.3	7.6	8.3	15.6	21.7
People who have been here longer should run the union							
Men	5.1	20.0	14.4	27.6	7.0	--	--
Women	5.9	6.9	5.3	11.4	11.1	11.1	15.0
Nothing about my job affects my union activity							
Men	46.2	4.0	47.8	26.8	52.6	--	--
Women	45.1	17.2	61.3	43.0	50.0	42.2	40.0
No answer							
Men	15.8	50.0	13.5	10.2	26.9	--	--
Women	12.1	42.0	21.9	19.4	36.8	28.6	34.1

In the same way, there is little difference between the opinions of men, whether active in union affairs or not, on the relation between union activity and their getting ahead on the job. But among women there is a difference, with women activists less interested in this relationship than any other group: "Union activity would have to give me a better chance to get ahead on the job."

	Men		Women	
	Activists (percent)	Less Active (percent)	Activists (percent)	Less Active (percent)
Postal	14	17	7	16
Meat cutters	57	50	40	36
Electrical	7	7	0	15
Custodial	43	42	20	25
Store workers	26	26	11	5
Hospital*	--	--	20	23
Garment*	--	--	17	24

*Only women members were included in the study.

Full data on job factors of most concern to rank and file members are presented in Table 4.4(B). Table 4.4(C) presents the data for members who have sought or held union positions.

UNION-RELATED FACTORS FOR INCREASING PARTICIPATION

The questionnaire responses in this section provide some valuable information to union leaders about changes that members suggest might increase their union participation.

By far the most important area for union action lies in educational programs. Where members were asked what the union could do to make it easier for them to participate, the top-ranking reply was that they want education programs. Second rank was given to wanting to know more about what people like themselves could accomplish in the union. Third choice was "I would like to learn some of the things a person needs to be a leader." Women tend to value all three more highly than men, although in the majority of unions both men and women responded with the same priorities. In every union, where either education programs or information on what could be accomplished was not first choice, it was a close second.

TABLE 4.4(B)

Job Factors of Most Concern to Members without Union Position

	Postal	Meat Cutters	Electrical	Custodial	Store	Hospital*	Garment*
Nothing about the job affects my union activity							
Men	38.9	7.1	45.2	23.5	44.4	--	--
Women	48.6	9.1	64.4	43.4	39.0	45.0	24.1
Supervisor should not make life hard for active unionists							
Men	27.8	57.1	28.6	23.5	11.1	--	--
Women	27.0	18.2	18.6	18.9	12.2	25.0	44.8
Union activity would have to give me a better chance to get ahead on the job							
Men	16.7	50.0	7.1	42.0	25.9	--	--
Women	16.2	36.4	15.3	24.5	4.9	22.5	24.1
People who hold important jobs in the shop deserve union position							
Men	5.6	35.7	7.1	18.5	11.1	--	--
Women	5.4	9.1	1.7	7.5	12.2	10.0	34.5
People who have been here longer should run the union							
Men	5.6	21.4	9.5	29.6	11.1	--	--
Women	5.4	9.1	5.1	5.7	19.5	12.5	20.7

*Only women members were included in the study.

TABLE 4.4(C)

Job Factors of Most Concern to Members Who Have Sought or Held Union Position
(in percents)

	Postal	Meat Cutters	Electrical	Custodial	Store	Hospital*	Garment*
Nothing about the job affects my union activity							
Men	50.6	0.0	48.8	33.3	63.0	--	--
Women	30.8	20.0	50.0	60.0	64.3	20.0	56.7
Supervisor should not make life hard for active unionists							
Men	32.9	28.6	31.7	38.1	11.1	--	--
Women	53.8	30.0	25.0	30.0	28.6	40.0	20.0
Union activity would have to give me a better chance to get ahead on the job							
Men	13.9	57.1	7.3	42.9	25.9	--	--
Women	7.7	40.0	0.0	20.0	10.7	20.0	16.7
People who hold important jobs in the shop deserve union position							
Men	3.8	42.9	14.6	14.3	14.8	--	--
Women	0.0	30.0	0.0	20.0	16.7	60.0	10.0
People who have been here longer should run the union							
Men	5.1	0.0	19.5	28.6	3.7	--	--
Women	7.7	0.0	25.0	40.0	0.0	0.0	6.7

*Only women members were included in the study.

One can and should speculate on the meaning of this high response to the cluster of choices that concern learning. It should be recalled that members also gave top rating, in the section on personal barriers to union participation, to the response that they would like more information about the union. In the section on job-related factors, first rank was given to a job problem which might be solved, at least in part, by skill training. Union members seem to have needs that education could help them meet, and they seem to prize the education aspect of union activity. The experience of Cornell's Industrial and Labor Relations (ILR) extension work and of those unions in the study that have their own well-developed education programs is that working men and women are proud of the programs their unions conduct even when they do not take part in them and that they respect and enjoy the learning activity when they can be part of it. For unions that undertake it, education is an activity with large benefits.

The areas of next importance to respondents in this study are the desire for recognition and for encouragement from union leaders. Men and women both tend to be more interested in recognition than in encouragement, but in every union fewer women assert the need for more recognition. Reasons for the smaller request may be that women are serving in lower-level posts and feel less deserving; or it may be that they are just less demanding, are used to serving without thanks. Location of union meetings appears as a problem of special importance to the meat cutters, electrical workers, and custodial assistants. The women of two unions, Postal and Electrical, indicate that child care would be useful in order for them to attend union meetings. Union social events have moderate appeal to members, particularly women.

Table 4.5(A) sets forth the ways members feel their unions could encourage greater activity.

Union Activists Compared with
Rank and File Members

What are the most important actions that unions could take to encourage less active members? In their own opinion, these members feel they need to know more about what they could accomplish if they were to become more active. The response makes good sense given the corresponding lack of information many of them reported they have about the

Union-Related Factors Respondents Believe Would Encourage Increased Participation
(in percents)

	Postal	Meat Cutters	Electrical	Custodial	Store	Hospital*	Garment*
Meetings held in more convenient place							
Men	17.3	59.0	50.0	35.5	11.3	--	--
Women	19.6	50.0	38.5	33.0	15.0	26.4	17.9
Meetings at a different time							
Men	18.2	15.4	13.3	18.5	20.8	--	--
Women	13.7	3.3	17.9	28.4	25.0	37.7	25.4
Child care arrangements in order to attend meetings							
Men	0.9	2.6	1.1	1.6	1.9	--	--
Women	19.6	10.0	5.1	4.5	5.0	13.2	7.5
Union should encourage me to be active							
Men	23.6	17.9	23.3	27.4	30.2	--	--
Women	25.5	6.7	14.1	30.7	8.8	18.9	20.9
I would like to know more about what is accomplished in the union by people like me							
Men	31.8	25.6	30.0	60.5	26.4	--	--
Women	52.9	36.7	30.8	38.6	30.0	43.4	31.3
Interested in union social events							
Men	14.5	7.7	8.9	27.4	15.1	--	--
Women	19.6	16.7	15.4	36.4	15.0	18.9	32.8
Would like education programs							
Men	43.6	25.6	34.4	48.4	35.8	--	--
Women	60.8	30.0	44.9	56.8	25.0	41.5	38.8
Like to learn some of the things a person needs to be a leader							
Men	26.4	15.4	22.2	42.7	13.2	--	--
Women	35.3	20.0	19.2	36.4	22.5	24.5	23.9
Union leaders need to give more recognition to people who do union work							
Men	30.0	20.5	24.4	34.7	28.3	--	--
Women	23.5	10.0	21.8	18.2	10.0	15.1	44.8
Union does not need to do anything more							
Men	14.5	7.7	8.9	5.6	11.3	--	--
Women	5.9	6.7	6.4	3.4	12.5	15.1	3.0
No answer							
Men	20.9	22.0	13.5	9.5	32.1	--	--
Women	12.1	40.0	18.8	10.2	29.8	15.9	26.4

*Only women members were included in the study.

union. It suggests that in spite of the union's newspaper, shop visits by business agents, steward training, and membership meetings, there is a need for more communication between rank and file members and the union leadership.

Women are more likely than men to be uncertain about their usefulness to the union. The uncertainty is bound to arise when so many easily identified posts are filled by men. Union leaders queried about the response are inclined to feel that if a person wants to accomplish something, she should begin by becoming informed, that there is always work for willing hands, and that there are ample avenues of information available. Both views have merit, and both have something to do with who the speaker is. The fact that both exist, however, strengthens the probability that there has been a breakdown in communication, especially between women rank and filers and the leadership

Next highest rating is given to education programs, particularly by women. It may be that lacking a clear idea of how they can be helpful to the union, rank and filers substitute the union action that would be most helpful to them. These unionists whose activity has not led to union position want to learn some of the things a person needs to know to be a leader. Although they also value encouragement and think union leaders should give it to them, they may be indicating by this response their own willingness to put forth the effort to learn useful skills, instead of simply waiting to be encouraged. A higher proportion of men than women is interested in acquiring leadership skills, and men are also more likely to want encouragement to become active. Considerably fewer members of either group think it important for union leaders to give more recognition to those who do union work.

A more convenient location for union meetings, while not as high a priority as some others, is clearly an important factor to less active members. For two unions both on Long Island, the Meat Cutters' and Electrical Workers', location is the most important factor. It is the members without a union post who are interested also in child care arrangements in order to attend union meetings. Table 4.5(B) describes the union factors of most interest to them.

When we turn to what more active members consider important for the union to do, the message seems to be that if union leaders wish them to be even more involved, there should be greater recognition for work already being done.

Education programs are equally or more important to union activists. However, they appear more certain than

106

TABLE 4.5(B)

Union-Related Factors of Most Interest to Members without Union Position
(in percents)

	Postal	Meat Cutters	Electrical	Custodial	Store	Hospital*	Garment*
Meetings held in more convenient location							
Men	21.6	60.0	47.6	36.6	3.7	--	--
Women	24.3	70.0	39.3	30.5	16.7	25.5	25.0
Child care arrangements in order to attend meetings							
Men	2.7	0.0	0.0	2.4	0.0	--	--
Women	24.3	20.0	6.6	1.7	4.2	14.9	8.3
Union should encourage me to be active							
Men	32.4	15.0	19.0	25.6	37.0	--	--
Women	29.7	20.0	14.8	35.6	10.4	17.0	22.2
Would like to know more about what is accomplished in the union by people like me							
Men	45.9	30.0	33.3	56.1	29.6	--	--
Women	62.2	70.0	32.8	39.0	33.3	40.4	27.8
Would like education programs							
Men	40.5	20.0	33.3	47.6	37.0	--	--
Women	59.5	40.0	45.9	57.6	20.8	40.4	36.1
Like to learn some of the things a person needs to be a leader							
Men	27.0	20.0	21.4	40.2	18.5	--	--
Women	24.3	30.0	18.0	33.9	16.7	21.3	16.7
Union leaders need to give more recognition to people who do union work							
Men	16.2	20.0	7.1	34.1	18.5	--	--
Women	21.6	0.0	19.7	13.6	8.3	12.8	36.1

*Only women members were included in the study.

107

rank and filers of what they could accomplish by giving
more time to the union. Instead, their emphasis is on acquiring leadership skills, with women tending to stress it
more than men.

A surprising finding is the importance to active
unionists of a more convenient location for meetings. Although their response here is generally not quite as high
as is that of less active members, it is even higher among
male electrical employees and women hospital workers. The
latter may equate greater union involvement with meetings
at union headquarters, rather than meetings held only at
their hospital work place. In every union the size of the
response by activists indicates that finding a convenient
location for meetings is an unsolved problem for most
unions. Postal, Garment, and Store Workers' Locals seem
to be solving it best.

The request for child care arrangements also contains
a surprise. Although child care is not registered as much
of a problem for active unionists, the men show interest
in it. One may speculate: Do the men feel they are not
seeing enough of their children? Would their wives accompany them to meetings if there were arrangements for the
children? Do they feel it would encourage more women--
and men--to become active in the union, or at least improve
meeting attendance?

Table 4.5(C) presents the responses of activists to
the question: What could the union do to make it easier
for you to participate?

MEMBERSHIP OPINION OF WOMEN'S PARTICIPATION

The final two questions to union members provide a
measure of the attitudes toward the involvement of women
in union affairs. While the responses are influenced by
the characteristics of each industry and the history of
the Local, the similarity of response is telling. In most
unions the men's attitude can be described as encouraging
to the "right" woman. Women are less discriminating and
enthusiastically endorse the greater involvement of women
generally.

Should More Women Run for Union Office?

Asked whether they think more women should run for
union office, the women answered with a resounding yes;

Union-Related Factors of Most Interest to Members Who Have
Sought or Held Union Position
(in percents)

	Postal	Meat Cutters	Electrical	Custodial	Store	Hospital*	Garment*
Meetings held in more convenient location							
Men	15.5	57.1	55.5	28.6	21.7	--	--
Women	7.7	33.3	35.3	33.3	10.3	40.0	10.0
Child care arrangements in order to attend meetings							
Men	0.0	7.1	2.5	0.0	4.3	--	--
Women	0.0	0.0	0.0	0.0	6.9	0.0	6.7
Union should encourage me to be active							
Men	18.3	28.6	27.5	28.6	26.1	--	--
Women	15.4	0.0	11.8	25.0	3.4	40.0	20.0
Would like to know more about what is accomplished in the union by people like me							
Men	25.4	21.4	22.5	61.9	17.4	--	--
Women	30.8	25.0	23.5	25.0	20.7	80.0	33.3
Would like education programs							
Men	46.5	35.7	27.5	57.1	34.8	--	--
Women	69.2	41.7	41.2	41.7	34.5	40.0	43.3
Like to learn some of the things a person needs to be a leader							
Men	26.8	7.1	25.0	61.9	8.7	--	--
Women	69.2	16.7	23.5	50.0	27.6	60.0	33.3
Union leaders need to give more recognition to people who do union work							
Men	36.6	21.4	45.0	52.4	43.5	--	--
Women	30.8	25.0	29.4	41.7	13.8	40.0	53.3

*only women members were included in the study.

the men's response was a less certain yes. In all unions
the overwhelming majority of women believe that more of
them should run for office, and in all unions more men
agreed than disagreed or were unsure. Men were less likely
to be unsure of their opinions than women were. Uncertainty by either group may indicate that members feel they
cannot give a blanket answer, that their answer would depend on the person, and perhaps on the office. Or it may
mean that these respondents are unsettled in their opinions
about the role of women. Possibly they are just fence-
sitters.

Note that in all but two unions the percentage of
women who believe women should not run for office is very
close to the reply of each Local to an earlier question,
"I am a woman and think men are better at union affairs."

Of all groups, men who are not actively involved in
the union are the least likely to think more women should
run for union office; activist women are the most sure they
should. Table 4.6 reports the answers to the question,
and Table 4.7 relates those answers to the level of activity of the respondents.

TABLE 4.6

Should More Women Run for Union Office?
(in percents)

	Yes		No		Not Sure		No Answer	
	Men	Women	Men	Women	Men	Women	Men	Women
Postal	68.0	82.1	19.2	1.8	12.8	16.1	10.1	3.4
Meat Cutters	39.1	64.4	34.8	20.0	26.1	15.6	8.0	10.0
Electrical	44.0	60.7	30.0	11.2	26.0	28.1	3.8	7.3
Custodial	45.8	71.4	30.5	9.9	23.7	18.7	4.4	7.1
Store	56.7	65.3	14.9	13.3	28.4	21.4	14.1	14.0
Hospital*	--	74.5	--	5.9	--	19.6	--	19.0
Garment*	--	73.0	--	12.2	--	14.9	--	18.7

*Only women members were included in the study.

110

TABLE 4.7

Level of Union Activity of Respondents Who Think
More Women Should Run for Office
(in percents)

	Rank and File Respondents		Union Activists	
	Men	Women	Men	Women
Postal	61.9	78.0	71.6	92.9
Meat Cutters	32.0	72.2	40.0	64.3
Electrical	44.9	58.6	48.8	64.7
Custodial	47.1	70.7	47.6	92.9
Store	58.1	65.6	59.4	69.7
Hospital*	--	71.1	--	100.0
Garment*	--	61.8	--	82.1

*Only women were included in the study.

Are Women as Interested in the Union?

There is greater unanimity among union members on the question of whether women take as much interest in the union as men. Whereas a 20-point difference between men and women was not unusual in answering the question of whether women should run for office, no union has that large a gap between men's and women's responses to this question.

Women firmly believe they are just as interested in the union as men. Men who hold union posts are the most likely to disagree.

In the Postal Union, respondents believe more women should run for office, while at the same time, except among "active" women, they register a considerably lower belief that women are as interested. On the other hand, male meat cutters are much more likely to think women are as interested as men but not that they should run for office. Table 4.8 reports the answers to the question, and Table 4.9 relates those answers to the level of activity of the respondents.

TABLE 4.8

Are Women as Interested in the Union as Men?
(in percents)

	Yes		No		Not Sure		No Answer	
	Men	Women	Men	Women	Men	Women	Men	Women
Postal	44.1	54.5	47.2	32.7	8.7	12.7	8.6	5.2
Meat Cutters	47.8	60.0	37.0	26.7	15.2	13.3	8.0	10.0
Electrical	36.4	64.1	49.5	23.9	14.1	12.0	4.8	4.2
Custodial	60.3	70.8	23.7	9.4	16.0	19.8	4.4	2.0
Store	59.1	73.3	21.2	16.2	19.7	10.5	15.4	7.9
Hospital*	--	82.7	--	3.8	--	13.5	--	17.5
Garment*	--	68.9	--	24.3	--	6.8	--	18.7

*Only women members were included in the study.

TABLE 4.9

Level of Union Activity of Respondents Who Think
Women Are as Interested in the Union as Men
(in percents)

	Without Union Position		Union Activists	
	Men	Women	Men	Women
Postal	47.6	48.8	41.0	69.2
Meat Cutters	60.0	72.2	26.7	57.1
Electrical	36.0	61.1	40.0	77.8
Custodial	62.5	69.4	55.0	86.7
Store	63.3	69.7	53.1	80.0
Hospital*	--	80.4	--	100.0
Garment*	--	69.7	--	68.3

*Only women were included in the study.

Age Correlates of Opinion on
Women's Participation

It is logical to ask whether there is an age correlation among union members on the question of women's ac-
tivism. A cross-tabulation of the data was prepared for
respondents who believe more women should run for office
and is set forth in Table 4.10. Age bears little relation
to opinion. The unique circumstances of each union, the
sex and racial composition of the membership, and the
level of union activity of all seem far better indicators
than the age of respondents. However, the age category
35-45 has the greatest consistency of opinion from union
to union. The correlation on women's interest in union
affairs shows no significant relationship between age and
opinion and is not exhibited.

TABLE 4.10

Ages of Respondents Who Think More Women
Should Run for Union Office
(in percents)

	Under 25		25 to 35		35 to 45		Over 45	
	Men	Women	Men	Women	Men	Women	Men	Women
Postal	80.0	100.0	55.6	68.0	68.0	92.9	72.1	90.9
Meat Cutters	33.3	75.0	21.4	75.0	57.1	57.1	20.0	50.0
Electrical	20.0	50.0	47.6	50.0	44.4	54.5	48.0	65.4
Custodial	28.6	a	43.8	66.7	58.1	64.0	42.6	74.2
Store	70.0	75.0	55.6	80.0	42.9	66.7	56.7	65.0
Hospital	b	50.0	b	72.7	b	66.7	b	90.9
Garment	b	a		75.0	b	62.5	b	76.9

aNo respondents under age 25.
bOnly women were included in the study.

DEMOGRAPHIC DISTINCTIONS BETWEEN ACTIVISTS
AND MEMBERS WITHOUT UNION POSITION

In order to understand the characteristics of union activists, and as an aid to leaders in identifying members most likely to be interested in and available for increased union activity, the activist respondents are described in terms of their age, marital status, age of children, position as sole support of the family, and opinion of their job-advancement opportunities.

Age

A majority of the men active in their unions are over age 45 in all unions except the Meat Cutters'. In that union, more than two-thirds of both men and women activists are 35 to 45 years old. Among hospital workers (women only), half are ages 35 to 45 and the rest are younger; none is over age 45. If we compare the proportion of any age group which is involved in union decision making with its representation as a percentage of all activists, we find that younger members, particularly men, are more active in relation to their numbers in the union than are older members. For example, in the Custodial Local, only a quarter of the male respondents over 45 years are active unionists, yet they represent 64 percent of "active" men; among women, just 21 percent of these over 45 years are active, yet they represent 71 percent of all female activists.

Women members under age 35 are far _less_ active than men of that age in three unions--Electrical, Custodial, and Store--but in the Postal Union they are more active; in the Meat Cutters' Union they are almost equally active; and women hospital workers under 35 are active in higher proportions than any comparable group of men and women in any other union.

The age of rank and file leadership presents a challenge: how to interest more of the younger members, especially women, in further commitment to the union. Postal workers, meat cutters, and hospital workers are exceptions. Table 4.11 presents the proportions of members whose activity has led to union position, in four age categories.

TABLE 4.11

Ages of Respondents Who Have Sought
or Held Union Position
(in percents)

	Under 25		25 to 35		35 to 45		Over 45	
	Men	Women	Men	Women	Men	Women	Men	Women
Postal	1.1	7.7	15.4	30.8	18.7	30.8	64.8	30.8
Meat								
Cutters	0.0	0.0	27.8	25.0	66.7	68.8	5.6	6.3
Electrical	2.2	0.0	17.8	0.0	24.4	22.2	55.6	77.8
Custodial	4.5	a	13.6	0.0	18.2	20.0	63.6	80.0
Store	2.7	8.8	16.2	2.9	16.2	17.6	64.9	70.6
Hospital	b	16.7	b	33.3	b	50.0	b	0.0
Garment	b	a	b	4.3	b	6.4	b	89.4

aNo respondents under age 25.
bOnly women were included in the study.

Marital Status

Women unionists who are divorced, separated, or widowed are the most likely to be active union members; next
are single women; least likely are married women. In only
one union (Store Workers') is the proportion of married
women who have achieved union position equal to their proportion in the membership, and in that union it is even
greater. But the percentage of activist women who are
separated or formerly married exceeds their percentage in
the membership of six unions; in the seventh, Hospital
Union, it is the single women who do. Women electrical
workers exhibit higher participation rates for both single
women and those formerly married or separated. However,
since there are very large numbers of married women respondents (63 percent in that union), more of their women
activists report being married (56 percent). In all unions
the proportion of married male respondents who are active
unionists is the reverse of women; men are more likely to
be active unionists if they are married. Table 4.12 describes the marital status of union members who have
served the union in an official capacity.

TABLE 4.12

Marital Status of Respondents Who Have Sought
or Held Union Position
(in percents)

	Married		Divorced, Separated, Widowed		Single	
	Men	Women	Men	Women	Men	Women
Postal	83.3	35.7	7.8	57.1	8.9	7.1
Meat Cutters	93.8	37.5	6.3	50.0	0.0	12.5
Electrical	93.2	55.6	4.5	27.8	2.3	16.7
Custodial	81.8	13.3	13.6	60.0	4.5	26.7
Store	86.5	57.9	2.7	28.9	10.8	13.2
Hospital*	--	33.3	--	16.7	--	50.0
Garment*	--	41.3	--	32.6	--	26.1

*Only women were included in the study.

Ages of Children

    The participation of women in union affairs appears
closely tied to the ages of their children rather than to
their own age. Participation rises with the age of children. The same pattern is generally true for men although
less dramatically. As one union president put it, apparently correctly, "Children do not mix well with union activity." (See Table 4.13.)

Sole Support

    Women who are the sole support of their households
are the majority of women activists in five of the seven
unions. Where men were included in the survey, four of
the five unions show that those who were the sole support
are also more active than men who are not, but the finding
has less import since the overwhelming majority of men are
married. The answers of female respondents raise questions about how these women cope with their responsibilities and whether there is some particular quality to
union activity that draws them from other uses of their
time. Table 4.14 indicates the level of activity of men
and women in the seven unions who are the sole support
of their families.

TABLE 4.13

Ages of the Children of Respondents Who Have Sought or Held Union Position
(in percents)

	Postal	Meat Cutters	Electrical	Custodial	Store	Hospital*	Garment*
Infant to 18							
Men	6.5	0.0	10.3	10.5	7.7	--	--
Women	0.0	16.7	0.0	14.3	4.0	0.0	0.0
Under 6 only							
Men	9.1	6.3	12.8	10.5	3.8	--	--
Women	16.7	0.0	0.0	0.0	4.0	25.0	0.0
6 to 18 only							
Men	24.7	37.5	17.9	21.1	30.8	--	--
Women	25.0	33.3	7.7	0.0	0.0	25.0	77.8
Under 18 and over 18							
Men	22.1	25.0	17.9	26.3	11.5	--	--
Women	16.7	16.7	23.1	28.6	20.0	0.0	0.0
Over 18 only							
Men	37.7	31.3	41.0	31.6	46.2	--	--
Women	41.7	33.3	69.2	57.1	72.0	50.0	48.5

*Only women were included in the study.

TABLE 4.14

Level of Union Activity of Respondents Who Are
the Sole Support of Their Households
(in percents)

	Rank and File Respondents		Union Activists	
	Men	Women	Men	Women
Postal	73.3	47.6	61.1	71.4
Meat Cutters	83.3	52.6	88.9	60.0
Electrical	62.5	43.1	72.1	55.6
Custodial	72.7	54.0	81.8	84.6
Store	63.9	46.3	70.3	38.9
Hospital*	--	60.0	--	50.0
Garment*	--	43.2	--	56.8

*Only women were included in the study.

Job-Advancement Possibilities

Women who believe they can advance on the job tend to
be more active in the union than those who think they cannot. Among men, however, those who think they can advance
on the job tend to be less active. Table 4.15 presents
the level of union activity related to respondents' assessment of advancement possibilities.

SUMMARY AND CONCLUSIONS

The opinions of union leaders in Chapter 2 appear to
be close to the mark. The top officers consider the principal reasons for women's relatively low level of union
responsibility to be the demands placed on women at home,
a fear of union responsibility, and women's overall tendency to think they are not as able as they really are.
Respondents themselves attribute their low participation primarily to home responsibilities or to a need to
feel more competent. In numerous responses, the view reflected is of lack of confidence in their ability, at this
time, to handle heavier union responsibility. One in ten
thinks men are better at union affairs, and twice that
number say they need to gain greater competence. Of the
first group, we can note that time may work a difference

in their belief but that until it has, these women are effectively unavailable to the union. Of the second group,
we can hope for better things. They are among the large
proportions which pushed education and union information
programs into first ranked responses. They want these
programs so that they can learn to handle union work.

TABLE 4.15

Level of Union Activity of Respondents Who Think
They Can Advance from Their Present Job
(in percents)

| | Rank and Filers | | Union Activists | |
	Men	Women	Men	Women
Postal	68.2	57.5	52.3	58.3
Meat Cutters[a]	--	--	--	--
Electrical	55.3	27.8	46.2	27.8
Custodial	55.2	43.8	61.9	66.7
Store	50.0	21.3	41.2	42.9
Hospital[b]	--	56.0	--	66.7
Garment[c]	--	--	--	--

[a]Question was not administered to this union.
[b]Only women were included in the study.
[c]Question does not apply well to most respondents as
they are skilled workers making the entire garment and
there is no job ladder.

It is the second group and a third, those two-women-
in-ten who report no reasons at all for not increasing
their union activity, to whom the unions can look for
volunteers to replenish their supply of committee members
and stewards. Before these women will become involved,
however, their responses have made it clear that they want
to know that their contribution is needed and important
to the union. They, more than men, value encouragement
from the union. They also value recognition.
The women appear to be realistic in making these requests of the union since the study shows that the higher
the union position, the fewer women are found in it. They
may have drawn the conclusion that there is not a great
deal of point in starting an activity for which women have
apparently been judged unsuitable.

Are women as interested in the union? Yes. Can their lower activity be explained by a lack of interest? It cannot. Among members who have never run for office or held a union position, women participate more heavily than men in voting in union elections, attending meetings, attending education and social events, and even in filing grievances. Fewer women than men state they are just not interested in union affairs. Overwhelmingly (almost 70 percent) women consider themselves as interested in the union as men, and about 50 percent of the men agree.

Although home responsibilities are the major reasons for low union activity on the part of only 24 percent of the female respondents, the effect is shown in the higher age of women activists and the higher age of their children. It is also reflected in the finding that, as a group, married women are the least likely to carry union responsibility. The most likely are divorced, separated, or widowed women, and second, those who are single. Further evidence of the effect of marriage is that women more than men would have to get their spouse's agreement to increased union activity. Perhaps an off-setting factor, and a sidelight on the effect of home responsibilities, is that fewer women than men would have to drop other outside activities in which they are interested in order to assume union tasks.

Since a majority of men in two unions and healthy proportions in the others (roughly 40 percent) think that more women should run for office, and since women agree with this overwhelmingly, it may be that the votes are there for enterprising women to collect. But first, women must have confidence in their own abilities, and the assurance that there is something concrete that they could accomplish for the union. And they need to begin.

THE LABOR UNION
WOMAN AS RANK
AND FILE LEADER

Women as union members are seen in one way by those
men and women in leadership positions and in another by
the women members themselves. In earlier chapters we examined attitudes of men and women based on over 1,500
questionnaires. It seemed important to validate and interpret these attitudes through interviewing a number of
activists, since there may be differences between individual thinking and that expressed in the aggregate.
What we found was that individual women unionists vary in
many ways, yet their words and the words of those who
know them and work with them reflect concerns and aspirations they have in common.

This chapter describes how top unionists and rank
and file women leaders perceive other women members, based
on interviews and written comments. Wherever possible we
shall let their own words reflect their feelings and shall
relate these to certain of the questionnaire findings reported in Chapter 4.

WOMEN UNIONISTS AS SEEN BY TOP LEADERSHIP

Interviews were conducted both with the presidents of
the seven study unions and with at least two other chief
officers or staff members. Where women were in these positions, they were selected.

Are Women Competent in Leadership Posts?

As we learned in Chapter 2, competency is no problem
for those women who accept responsibility. Murray Gross,

general manager of the Dress and Waistmakers Joint Council
and Joint Board, stated it this way for his union:

> All our women leaders are good. They have
> no problems of competence in any direction.
> I would trust them with any kind of job at
> all. Women can get along with anyone.
> They have no trouble getting along with
> men. There is a tradition of long stand-
> ing though, that there are stages to union
> position. Age and length of time in the
> union are steps.

He described the typical woman leader as "happily married,
no young children, or determinedly nonmarried. Children
do not mix well with union activity. Women who are returning after their children are taken care of are the
best bet. . . . Younger, unmarried women also become
very interested in the union. But they get married."

President James Trenz of Local 463, Electrical Workers, adds his experience: "Our active women are not only
competent (sometimes more so than the men) but also well
motivated. They give time and make sacrifices. It's
true more women do come to meetings. I think our women
rank and filers _are_ more interested than the men."

The postal workers have used women in organizing campaigns in the suburbs. Women have had to persuade large
numbers of men to join the union. President Morris Biller
describes the results:

> We have three women organizing in Carney,
> New Jersey. They have terrific spirit.
> With them, it's like it was in the old
> days; something seems to have vanished
> from the spirit of the men. These women
> have no problem at all in organizing men.
> They organized 200 in a week. They can
> sit down with them, talk naturally in
> their language. They relate to the people
> they are trying to organize.

Hospital Workers' vice-president Doris Turner sees it
this way: "Women are more thorough than men. They stick
to things more. But men are more experienced and more
sure of themselves."

Two union leaders mention the special qualities
minority group women bring to the union:

I've found black women are more independent. Maybe they were forced to be, on
account of the early circumstances of
their life. They are not unpleasant or
aggressive; there are some of the sweet-
est people you ever want to meet. But
they know what they want. They take advantage of opportunities. They come to
meetings percentagewise more than men.
They want to improve themselves.

In the words of the other: "Black women seem more outgo-
ing. This is probably based on their background of fighting for what they have at every step of the way."
President Michelson of the Store Workers' Union makes
this thoughtful observation: "The competence of the women
varies, you really can't generalize. Many have very great
competence. The most important single factor to their
competence is their motivation."

Motivation and Sacrifices of Women Leaders

Leaders must find a reward in service, it is felt.
The job is demanding. They are at everyone's beck and
call, and the hours are long. There is one problem to
handle after another.
In the Meat Cutters' Union, Irving Stern, director
of organization, sees the hours as a special obstacle for
women. "The amount of time a leader has to give is a real
problem. It does require sacrifice. Traveling around at
night, for instance, is a necessary part of it."
John Crumedy, president of the Custodial Assistants'
Union, says: "It's hard to lead. It takes a lot of time.
A leader should be involved with his membership. A person
who is going to be an officer has to be available to the
members at all times. It's not that easy to find someone."
Another leader puts it this way:

Most people here, regardless of how they
started, get bitten by the bug. You have
to be interested in the union because even
without killing yourself, taking it easy,
a staff person spends ten hours a day with
no trouble. We get on the road before 8
a.m. when the men come on, then there are
the night meetings. I'd say 12 hours at

least. But it gets to be such a part of
everyone, they just do it.

Leon Davis, president of the National Hospital Union, reflects on the problem:

> The financial lure is not there. In some
> cases staff jobs pay less than a person's
> regular job. They must love the work to
> take it on. To encourage rank and file
> leaders for a staff job if they are tapped,
> they get a one-year period with a leave of
> absence from the job. But the biggest
> problem we have is securing and developing
> leadership.

To this Doris Turner of the Hospital Union adds, "Women
are involved in growing numbers on the union staff, but
there is one job we can hardly fill, organizer. The nature of that job is very demanding. Night and day work.
This makes even active members reluctant to take it on."
    What motivates those women who have become leaders?
What makes the job worth the sacrifices? In only one
case did a top male leader mention the motivation that
rank and file women leaders rated most important when
they were asked the same question: the satisfaction of
developing their own special abilities and using them.
    Women in leadership, however, often use the same
words as rank and file women leaders when they discuss
women's motivations. Edith Hammer (IUE) mentioned that
knowing she was helping people was an important part of
her love for the work. Gloria Ford of the Store Workers'
Union cites this as well as other reasons:

> I find active women are older, in their
> 40's and on, whose children are grown.
> They are looking for something to do that
> will be helpful. Some are active in the
> union because they know it is important
> and no one else is stepping forward to do
> it. But women want recognition too. They
> are often more competent than the men, and
> they are willing to make the sacrifices
> they must.

Ida Torres, vice-president of that union, feels that the
union relationship can only be built on love of the union,
"sincere caring for it and for the members."

On the other hand, one woman in a key position described her own rise in the union in these words: I knew
what I wanted and where I wanted to go. I bided my time,
never gave ground."

What do the men think motivates their activist women?
"Interest in the union," is cited over and over. From
District Council 37: "The union is interesting and important to city workers. Things were so bad before the union
came in. For us, it is THE union. We are willing to work
hard. What motivates women? Interest in the union."
Women also want the union to function well. Philip Selig-
man of the Postal Union says, "Women become active because
they think the union is not doing enough. The women are
very good. They fight for their seniority and rights."
Other leaders express the same thought: "They want the
committees to work, so they get involved." "We have had
many problems with our management but have at last decided
to come together and attempt to resolve some of them. Consequently, the women's interest is high." Status is a reward another union president believes women derive from
their union activity: "They want equal status in the company, in the work place. The union provides an opportunity
for people to have the appearance of this, to get recognition from the managers. They meet big shots. Talk to them
as peers." Although he regards status as most important,
he added three other motives that he feels are relevant:
First, women have a special need to do something to help
someone; second, the union is useful in getting to know
people and making friends (many women in this Local live
alone and their social lives are likely to be limited to
the job); third, they like to be "in the know," to be
where the decisions are made.

President Leon Davis believes that one factor moti-
vating women in his union is the organization's stand on
key issues for hospital workers, including support for the
Equal Rights Amendment and extension of protective labor
laws to men as well as women. This wider aspect of union
activity was noted by A. H. Raskin[1] as an important ele-
ment in the spirit of District 1199. Davis is quoted
speaking to the off-job issues that are important to his
membership, "We will raise high the banner of struggle in
the fight against poverty, discrimination, ignorance,
hate, and war." Raskin found, and we concur, that fighting for these larger community issues added to the members' sense of self-respect, their appreciation of union-
won gains, and their sense of participation in collective
action.

The one comment that most eloquently states what we found to be the primary motivation of rank and file women leaders was made by President Michelson of the Store Workers' Union: "The union provides opportunities for men and women to exercise their talents. What else do you do with your life?"

Leadership Routes Most Available to Women

In most unions, leaders come from the ranks. Even for staff positions that require special expertise, such as director of the pension fund or education director, unions prefer to look first within their own membership to fill the post. There is some movement between unions, instances where a person will be hired away from one to work for the other, but these movements are far more rare than in business. As one president explains it:

> Union leadership for us invariably comes
> from the rank and file activity. Why?
> Because those are the people who are well
> known to the members. They have played
> key roles in crises of the union and they
> can rally the members to be supportive in
> other crises.

How do leaders go about locating able rank and filers to move into positions of union responsibility? How do rank and filers make themselves visible and attractive candidates for these positions? In discussing these questions, it became clear that leaders feel that women have characteristics that appear to limit their effectiveness.

Yet in unions with a high female membership, it is a matter of importance that potential women leaders be trained for increased responsibility. A woman commenting on the situation in her Local looked ahead, "As the men retire, we need to have women trained to replace them. Women are the major one source for leadership that we have."

The avenues to union leadership are much the same in all the unions: to attend meetings, speak up, and get elected shop steward. Edith Hammer advises that "there is always room to move up. You don't need any special background. Run for steward, for committee positions. The thing is to get elected."

Running for shop steward is regarded by other women who made it to the top as the best way of helping the union while at the same time demonstrating leadership qualities. Many shops have poor stewards, men who do not defend the workers or who are not diligent in union business. The counsel of one woman is to build on this situation:

> The best way up is to challenge these stewards. You don't get into a situation of trying to bump a steward just because you are ambitious. Conditions are so bad sometimes, a woman wouldn't need to be ambitious. It's the conditions that will make her so mad she will go ahead and run. Then there she is.

From DC 37, John Toto, director of the White-Collar Division, has this advice for emerging leaders:

> Attend meetings for a start. Listen to the people there. If you hear someone who makes a lot of sense, go over and say, "Let's you and I volunteer for this." Get used to talking. Get up and give reports. If you're a committee member, make sure that it isn't just the chairman who gives the whole report.
> Then if there's a vacancy, the Executive Board will look to these people--they are dependable. We want to get rank and file people active. Once found, they are like gold.
> The key is coming to meetings. You can't get appointed to a committee if you don't.

President Crumedy of the Custodial Assistants' Union underscores that advice with his observation:

> I wouldn't appoint anyone just because they asked to be on a committee. It's not that easy. Meetings are only every other month, that's not too much, and if I see some woman attending all the meetings, then I would appoint her. I try to get those involved who haven't had a chance before.

The qualities looked for are reliability, good judgment, ability to make decisions and to inspire confidence, and a willingness to accept the demands of the work.

> We look for a woman to move up who is some-
> one respected more than liked. When we
> went looking for a field representative,
> we looked for a mature, reliable woman.
> She was the first and she was very good.

> Leaders emerge by attending meetings,
> training courses including that for shop
> steward, joining committees. Then by be-
> coming committee chairmen and stewards.
> BEING ALWAYS ON CALL. That's the route
> the men take who move up to union rep and
> that's the route women have to take.

Gloria Johnson, education director of the IUE, believes that "experience is the basis for leadership. Women are very competent, but they need to get that experience."
President Abondolo of the Meat Cutters' Union also emphasizes experience as essential for holding union posts. Education programs are a mainstay of his union but,

> It is experience that gives confidence and
> builds leaders. Formal education is not a
> requirement. It wasn't for me. Experience
> in union activity, on committees, and in ne-
> gotiation is crucial for leadership develop-
> ment. And some women negotiate very well.

Leaders are aware that sometimes eager rank and filers may be seen by those holding office as potential threats. The problem is not one that presidents of Locals admit as a major concern, but they believe that women can "get hurt" in jockeying for union posts. One officer reports:

> There's a lot of competitiveness in the
> union, fears of being displaced. Members
> would like to have staff jobs, and the
> staff all come out of the ranks. I've
> seen the staff smash an Executive Board
> member who stands out too much from the
> rest.

Ida Torres of the Store Workers' Union suggests that this kind of tension is unnecessary. "Women don't need to

displace men. If men reflect the needs of women as well
as men, there is no need to replace them."
     Infighting over a limited number of posts is a poten-
tial problem. "After all," one president asks, "how many
vice-presidents can you make?" He sees the solution in
terms of union expansion. "The best hope for women is in
organizing where there is no union yet. This is a wide
open field. If this avenue is not exploited, there could
be a leadership crisis." He considers that the force pro-
pelling the union to grow is directly related to the degree that women seek to rise, both in the union and into
positions of equality generally.
     But others see the problem in more traditional terms.
They see women as inexperienced, unwilling to compete, and
lacking in confidence. When women have shown they have
the ability, these leaders say they see no reason why
women should not function on every level of the union.
But they must prove themselves first.

> I have watched the more interested of the
> women and at least half of them could take
> more responsibility than they do. They
> could function at a higher level.

> The biggest problem is the women themselves.
> They accept the stereotyped roles of men and
> women. Very few seem to think they can make
> it. They need more confidence. They need
> experience too, but those who at least have
> some confidence, you can help.

One officer bemoans the increase in the female membership
of his union because women don't run for union posts the
way men do. "They don't want to compete. We practically
have to force women to be shop stewards." He went on to
comment, "You have to encourage the women all right.
There are always plenty of men lined up for vice-president."
     Another deplores the shyness of his activist women,
even those who are the most capable. "Women are not speaking up on Steward Councils as they should. I know they
have a lot to say. In small groups they speak effectively."
     Leaders in still other unions applauded the recogni-
tion by women of the importance of gaining competence.
The president of one union, disappointed that its women
members rated their need for competence lower than others,
commented that the response was a reflection of a poor
job done by the steward or shop chairman. "He can't be

doing much or members would have a healthier respect for the job." One union representative approved the desire for competence expressed by women questionnaire respondents but not their need for more information about the union before becoming active. "That's the kind of answer that just leans on someone else. When they say they want to feel more competent, it means they are willing to do something for themselves." This man and his associates complained further about the women's desire for more information:

> We have so many ways we get information out. The paper, new members classes, contract and welfare-pension booklets, meetings, prenotification by mail and through union reps of events and meetings, committees, shop visits. Why would women say they need more information?

The president suggested, "Maybe we're not giving them the information they want to hear."

Male Attitudes toward Women

The opinions of union officers and staff also were solicited on the attitudes that rank and file men hold toward women in union leadership. Male leaders were less sanguine than the women about the willingness of men to accept female leadership. One estimated that it takes four or five years to develop leaders. He reports resistance from the men when he starts to train a woman.

> I want the women to be more active, but it's hard to buck the opinions of the men. I decided that the best way to break through their prejudice would be for me to just appoint women from the ranks. And that's what I'm doing now. I think when you expose men to competent women, it will begin to give them some sense of maturity.

Men will vote for women for union-wide posts if they are known to the stewards and have "proved themselves." However, most officers believe it is harder for men in the shops to accept a woman as the person they turn to, as the person with the authority to deal with management.

Women are regarded as a "drag" by many rank and file men.
Remarks at union meetings, spoken in a joking manner, actually express and probably reinforce traditional stereotypes. When a woman puts forward a point of view different from the others, according to one leader, the men will
call out, "That's the women for you." Or men will comment, "They don't back you up."

The officers of two unions revealed the contradic-
tions that appear more common than outright bias. In discussing the routes for advancement available to women, one
leader reported that no woman had ever expressed an interest in running for the post of shop chairman. However, in
the preceding interview, which was with a woman in that
very union, she had revealed that this was exactly the
position she was planning to run for, and she regarded it
as a logical post on the way up the union leadership ladder. In the other case, the head of a union division
stated that, in his judgment, there is no resentment of
women by the men. "We're a very open union. Always looking for people." In the next breath, however, he doubted
that a woman would be eligible for a foreman's job.

The job factor is one about which rank and file men
appear to their union leaders to be ambivalent if not
hostile.

> Men resent women shifting into "men's jobs."
> The women were unhappy about the different
> job categories, but not too many of them
> complained. Then the law came along and we
> just had to tell the men that if a woman
> can do the work and wants to, she's entitled.

> We have a woman now in one of these cate-
> gories. Automatically, the guys don't
> like it. "She's going to drag down
> standards."

In another union, it was the Local that opened up certain
jobs to women. They had to fight to do it, but were successful. The result was that after a while the men tended
to drift away from the newly sex-integrated jobs. In the
opinion of this leader, "I don't think you can get men to
work on the same jobs. You can mix blacks and whites, but
it's hard to mix men and women." He thinks there is a
basic desire among both men and women to work at separate
jobs. Openings for all jobs in his shops are posted, yet
women do not apply. In this instance, however, the men

131

do not necessarily earn more money, "they may even earn less. But it is true that the men tend to look down their noses at the women's work."

Job shifting appears to be important to many women in spite of the problems of competition and relationships with co-workers. Addie Gasman, a woman store worker who entered the traditionally male job of commission sales-person in furniture, said of her experience, "It is tough, but it's worth it. I wouldn't have it any other way." In the IUE, Gloria Johnson reports, "A lot of women are push-ing for women to take the on-job-training apprentice pro-gram even if they don't enter it themselves. That's a first step."

How do rank and file women feel about women in lead-ership posts in the union? Women leaders think that women have just as much confidence in a woman as in a man. They understand that some men may resent them, but for the most part they think such resentment is not widespread. In the Garment Union, a high number of women respondents said they think men are better at union affairs. Commented Secretary-Manager Breslow of Local 22:

> It would have been higher in the old days.
> Then it was hard to be accepted as an offi-
> cer unless a woman looked and talked like
> a man, even though ours has always been an
> industry with a majority of women. There
> is still a lot of bias, and it exists
> among women too. If a man and woman ran
> on a secret ballot, the man would get it
> even in a female shop.

WOMEN UNIONISTS SPEAK FOR THEMSELVES

Thirty-nine interviews were conducted by women rank and file leaders who had been selected by the presidents of the seven unions cooperating in the study. These in-terviewers were stewards, committee members, or members of local Executive Boards. Each union nominated 2 such women, but subsequently 2 of the 14 were not able to par-ticipate, bringing the total number of interviewers to 12. Each of the seven study unions provided the names of four rank and file women leaders to be interviewed in this phase of the project. Women did not interview mem-bers of their own union.

The Interviewing Experience

The interviewers asked to participate in this phase of the study approached their assignment with trepidation. A one-day training program helped equip them to conduct the interviews, and each was provided with interview schedules, supplementary questionnaires, and the names of two women they were to contact. None had ever done interviewing before. Although we were impressed with the poise of the women, they reported to us later that if they looked at ease during the training session, it was not a true guide to their feelings.

All described their nervousness when they phoned to arrange appointments with the women assigned to them. Many went to a great deal of trouble--phoning, not finding the person in, calling back, finding the person had moved. Some interviews were held during the day, but many were at night and often far from where the women lived. Since it was January, the interviewers faced bad weather as well as travel to parts of the city some did not know at all.

When the interviews were completed, the 12 women attended an evaluation session to discuss their experiences. The first response, a unanimous one, was that they were surprised to find that the women they interviewed had been just as nervous as they. One had kept her interviewer waiting an hour and a half because she had so dreaded the interview. When it was over, both women found they had enjoyed it.

The women spoke principally, however, of the respect they felt for most of those they met. All were strangers to one another, but the bond of union sisterhood proved a strong one. The unselfishness of many of these women, their desire to help others, and their stories of abuse and triumph moved and inspired the interviewers.

They also learned something about other unions and other ways of approaching similar problems. A stalwart unionist, Louise Evans of District 1199, commented that she discovered "other unions than 1199 are interested in equal rights and better lives for their members. I liked learning that." A black woman found that "one woman I interviewed was white--and I loved her. This I liked. I could have kissed her. She has the same goals in life, finding a better way of helping people."

Postinterview conversations were part of the pleasure. While the interviewers had worried that there would not be enough time, it turned out not to be a problem. Their "subjects" liked the interview experience and brought out cake and coffee as a prelude to further talk.

"Women Are Less Active Than They Should Be"

Women active in the union deplored the fact that other
women do not take more part. They are aware of women's two
"jobs"--work and home--but felt that home responsibilities
often were used as an excuse: "They have time to go to the
hairdresser but not to come to a union meeting" and "Part-
timers don't come to meetings, but if they are asked to
work overtime, they have time for that."

Some women sense that men's attitudes toward union
activity seem different. They regard men as having more
time, but also "for the men, this is part of their bread
and butter. They are going to find out what it is all
about." There was disagreement here with the implication
of this statement that women do not consider their jobs
bread and butter. Seeking another reason, since all
agreed that a great many women work because they have to,
one woman offered the explanation that "working-class
women don't look ahead. Making money interests them and
that's all. Let someone else worry about how things go."
Others added:

> Women are complacent, willing to let the men
> run the union. It's because they don't come
> to meetings that the men take over.

> We have the idea that men are supposed to
> be leaders, to be the president, vice-
> president. Maybe a woman secretary is all
> right.

"Women Don't Think about Moving Up"

The interviewees were asked if they thought it would
bring women to meetings if they thought a woman could be
president or hold other chief union posts. There was
unanimous agreement that such expectations would make a
significant difference.

Two contradictory beliefs were expressed by women
interviewed. On the one hand, many active women unionists
considered there were no barriers to women's participation
in the union. On the other hand, the idea of a woman as
president or other chief officer was tenuous and even for-
eign. This contradiction was explained by the women interviewers:

> The women we talked with were speaking in
> terms of shop steward and lower-level
> leadership. That's true. There are no
> unusual barriers there. They were not
> thinking in terms of higher office.

> Women don't think about moving up. They
> want to help the underdog, those workers
> who can't speak up for themselves.

Some women appear to want to move ahead in the union
and some do not. One woman who does suggested that the
reason others do not might be related to their being un-
aware of opportunities for education in union skills.
She is enrolled in a Cornell program in labor studies:
"To go to the Labor College, all I had to do was ask the
union and they agreed to send me."
The problem that was the major obstacle for all the
women was that the posts at the top are already filled.
As one woman said in defending both the high interest of
women and the good faith of her union, "Woman are not
represented enough, but I have to say why. The jobs are
filled by men."
Some unions have more room than others for advancement without displacing anyone. The women assessed the
opportunities in their own unions, and we found their
assessment paralleled the statements of leaders of those
unions as reported earlier in this chapter.

"There's No Reason a Woman Can't Be a Supervisor"

There was considerable ambivalence about advancing on
the job if that meant moving into a management position.
One of the interviews was trying out for a new job with
supervisory rank. This job was a great challenge for her
both as an individual and as a woman. She felt she had to
prove that women can successfully hold such posts:

> I kill myself in the supervisor's job be-
> cause I feel a woman should be able to do
> this job and a woman should be able to get
> it if the company decides to make it per-
> manent. I tell the men, "I can lift just
> as much as you can if not more." The men
> say I'm crazy to do this. But I'll do any-
> thing to rise. I can't go any higher from
> where I am now unless I tackle this.

While the other women were sure that a woman could do it ("There's no reason a woman can't be a supervisor"), they were hesitant about moving into management if it meant leaving the union.

> You have no job security if you're a supervisor.

> I've always been a union member wherever I've worked. I like to solve problems, to be able to help someone. I like working with union people because they are concerned with helping others.

> I never take the upgrading tests because I'm at the top for my union's jurisdiction. I think many women don't shoot higher because they don't want to leave our union. I just love that Blue-Collar Division.

"My Husband Was Not Pleased at First, But He Came Around"

Most of the 39 women interviewed did not depend on the encouragement of their husbands. Twenty-six of the women were married at the time they first became active in their unions. Only eight of these reported that their husbands encouraged their activity, and seven of the husbands of these women were themselves active in their own unions. Of the other husbands, most were displeased but had no choice but to go along with it. Remarks such as, "My husband thinks I'm crazy," and "My husband thinks I'm too involved," were mixed with severe judgmental statements, for example: "The men want you to lean. They reject women who are independent." Most husbands did not seriously object since it was something their wives saw as a benefit.

> He was not pleased--so much time taken from home. But he said, "If it's for your benefit, it's okay with me."

> My husband said that the job held no glory (shop steward), but if I wanted to do it, he would help me manage.

> At first he objected but after a while he came to accept it.

136

There were other responses as well. One woman con-
cealed her union involvement, covering her absence from
home by saying she was on a different shift. "He couldn't
believe I had done this." Now she would like to spend
more time with the union, but her husband says there is
not enough time for the two of them. She has compromised
on the issue. The former husband of one woman leader ob-
jected to the time she spent at the Labor College, accus-
ing her of neglecting the child over whom she has custody:
"But if I were to work overtime, I'm sure he would approve
of my spending the evenings out."
     For the most part, the active women unionists did not
consider their husbands' opinions as a barrier to their
involvement, and the men grew accustomed to their wives'
roles in the unions. Some men were proud of their wives
when they began union activity and others became proud
later.

                Children Were Not a Problem

     How do the women who have children manage to combine
union work with the responsibilities of child care? Of
the 39 women, more than half had young children when they
first became active in their unions. The largest number
depended on the assistance of their mothers; the preferred
second was using a friend or sitter to care for the children. In some cases the oldest child took care of younger
siblings. Often, if no one were available, the women
brought their children to union meetings. Some women made
a habit of bringing their children with them. One union
leader commented that her mother always brought her to
union meetings; she thinks that it was a good way to grow
up: "I'm a daughter of the union all right." In only
one case did a woman report that her husband always took
the responsibility.
     In some cases, women went to considerable trouble to
arrange for child care, but found the extra trouble was
worth it.

          I had three small children, but was able
          to manage without family to leave them
          with. I strongly believe that if you are
          determined, you will find a way.

          I had to pay a baby-sitter extra money in
          order to attend meetings. When I could

not get someone to watch my daughter, I
would take her with me. It was well
worth it.

No problem. There was always someone.

What Motivates Women to Become Active Unionists?

This question was central to our inquiry. We approached it by means of three interview questions and administration of a supplementary attitudinal questionnaire
which each person interviewed was asked to complete.
The results of the questionnaire and the responses
to the questions lead us to the conclusion that these
women seek and find in union activity a sense of satisfaction and fulfillment. They accomplish something they believe to be worthwhile. They are proud of their ability
to develop and employ their talents; this is the prime
motivation of the women interviewed. Loyalty to the
goals of the union, accompanied by allegiance to group
goals generally, is the second motivation. Close behind
this is the wish to participate in interesting and chal-
lenging activity: This wish many cannot fulfill in their
jobs. Fourth is the social aspect of union activity, the
chance to get out more and make new friends. Of somewhat
lower importance was the desire to lead and be recognized.
The desire to be independent, to avoid being bossed by
others, was the least important reason women gave for
their union activity. Appendix D presents the supplementary attitudinal questionnaire.
One interview question designed to discover motivation was: "What do you think was the most important reason or event that led to your present work in the union?"
Some women related specific events such as strikes or organizing campaigns which triggered their union activity.
More responded with statements of what they hoped to find
through union involvement.

I was eager to see what I could do and to
better myself and advance in some way.

I got involved without planning to, but
wanted to see women have something.

When I first started to work, there was no
union in my shop. I didn't like the way
the workers were being treated.

I wanted to see the union grow. I wanted
people to see the union the way I do; it
is a big part of their lives. It is very
important to fight for other people even
if you get in a lot of trouble with the
boss. But I enjoy fighting for someone.

I was a founder of this particular union
in my place of work. The conditions in
the shop were bad. I make sure all our
members hear about the benefits the union
has brought.

Workers always asked me to help them with
their problems. I wanted to help people
as much as I could. I enjoy it.

The workers needed someone not afraid to
speak up, to act as their spokesman.

I think going to classes and learning how
the union functions were the most important events that got me interested.
(Seven women attributed their present
level of union activity to courses or
seminars.)

I love to work with people. I've found
that some people have problems and don't
know how to present them properly. From
time to time I see that management and
union members are trying to say something
to each other, but they don't know how to
express themselves to one another. I get
pleasure when the members' problems are
solved.

I saw other workers were not aware of what
the union could do for them. I felt in
myself that they were afraid to speak out,
that they needed someone to do this for
them, and I decided to be the one.

I like helping people and I like people.
It irks me to see anyone, especially
women, being taken advantage of.

Another question asked was: "What do you like best about
working in the union?" The women reported that they most
enjoy helping other people and receiving the feeling they
are doing something for others. They enjoy the chance to
better themselves. They regard the work as interesting
and rewarding both in itself and in providing a chance to
be a leader in a worthwhile effort. Some characteristics
of union leadership the women found most rewarding were:

- settling grievances and trying to keep peace in
  the shop
- communicating with workers, getting to know them,
  solving their problems
- organizing activities in the union
- presenting ideas to delegates' meetings and the
  challenge this involves
- earning the respect of fellow workers and management
- getting workers what is due them, the satisfaction
  of doing the steward's job well
- learning all the time
- seeing what women can accomplish under proper
  leadership
- contributing back to the union something for all
  it has contributed to you
- knowing what is going on

A total of 17 of the 39 women interviewed responded
that a sense of achievement and helping people was what
they liked best. Other answers related to the social as-
pects, recognition, and the interesting nature of union
activity. The women also value contact with higher officers in their unions. As a hospital delegate remarked:
"What I like best is that there are always opportunities;
of course, I'm speaking for my union. I also like the
togetherness and friendship that our union president and
vice-president offer the members."
The importance of individual recognition was high
among questionnaire responses of active members as reported in Chapter 4. It is not news to union leaders,
although few of them commented on it, perhaps because it
is obvious to them that it is recognition that repays
workers for freely given union effort. The need for
recognition at first seems less when we examine the words
of those interviewed. Friendship, a feeling of camarade-
rie, and respect are more often the qualities they seem
to seek. However, if the satisfaction of doing a worth-

while job well is the main motivation for women activists, they also feel the need to have this accomplishment validated by someone else. The "someone else" is the leader.

The reply of a meat wrapper sums up the feelings of most:

> What did I like best? The closeness of the members. The respect that's received for your efforts. My own fulfillment in being involved and getting a job done. I feel very rewarded in the Credit Union by the happiness expressed by those who have a savings account they would not have had without my starting them.

The sense of accomplishment and recognition of that accomplishment are closely intertwined.

The importance of encouragement to less active women was another response often found in the questionnaires, as reported in Chapter 4. Interviews verified that encouragement by a union official, usually the union representative, was the way 15 of the active women unionists began their own union involvement. On the other hand, 24 of these rank and file women leaders started without encouragement from the union; 8 were curious to know more about the union and began volunteering, while 16 saw something that needed to be done and decided they would do it. After requests for education programs, the major request of rank and filers who answered the questionnaire discussed in the preceding chapter was: "I would like to know what could be accomplished in the union by people like me." The interview findings we have discussed highlight this need.

The third of the interview questions concerning the motivation of women activists was: "If another woman were to ask your advice on getting involved in the union, would you recommend it? Why?"

The answers demonstrate the loyalty and allegiance women have to their unions. The number one reply was: By becoming involved in the union a woman would help to build a stronger organization, one that would be better for everyone. Similar reasons reappear in the responses of rank and file women leaders in each of the study unions. Some examples are given:

> A working woman should know about these things. With knowledge, she can help others as well as herself.

When you are a part of something and know
what is going on, you can help others.

She could do something for the union. She
could learn more.

I think women should have more to say
about how the union is run and should be
run. There are more women union members
and she should get active.

It's good to know what is going on.

I would recommend it because of the part
labor has played through the years--jobs,
job security, pension, and other benefits.

The union is a place for all women. It is
not just a one-man show.

All women should be active. Since the
greater percentage of the membership is
male, women's participation is needed to
elevate the status of women.

Every lady should get to know about our
union and the problems it faces. Every-
body should do her part.

Being involved gives her a chance to implement changes and see how the union is
run from within.

Union involvement is interesting, stimulating, and tends to keep you young by
being active.

It is a good way of meeting people and
getting out.

You must have a union to get what is
right. Also it is a way of getting
ahead.

Women can and are doing a better job
than the male union leaders.

The emphasis placed on more information about the union, more understanding of what women could accomplish, and more education programs--three critically important responses of the questionnaire distributed to rank and filers--is not characteristic of women looking for excuses, as some top leaders seemed to feel. These are major needs of people who are or want to be active.

Do You Believe There Is Resistance from Men or Women to Your Leadership Role?

Most of the women interviewed believed that neither men nor women have much, if any, resentment toward women who are active in the union. However, seven felt men definitely resent women leaders; three thought women preferred male leaders; and one woman believed both men and women prefer men. Special comments noted that there was more resentment of a woman leader because of her youth than because of her sex, that formerly there was more resistance from women but because of the women's movement this has changed, that seniority is more important than a person's sex.

In the evaluation session conducted with the interviewers, one explanation offered for the relatively low union activity level of women was that women do not feel they carry as much weight as men. There was agreement that this represented the opinions of many women, but the interviewers disagreed with the statement. Their experience is that women carry as much weight as men--when they make it their business to do so.

Since there were so many expressions of confidence in the ability of women and in their concern for union goals, the interviewers were asked if they thought the union would be better off if women ran it. The consensus was that women would do just as well but not necessarily better. Women could take on the job provided they had the opportunity, training, and experience. Right now the group felt that they do not have the experience, particularly in the area of negotiating. "We need to learn the ropes." But, countered another, "How are you going to learn the ropes? Women are not on the inside; they have no power." Still another said, "You need a man to negotiate against the company's big-time lawyers, to go to Washington and Albany and present the union's case. It would take too much out of a woman. And jail. Could women take it?" A spontaneous yes was the group's answer.

143

SUMMARY AND CONCLUSIONS

The words reported in this chapter are those of men and women who care about trade unionism, their own union as an organization, and about its members. These union leaders were asked to consider the specific role of women, but their priorities appear to be clear: the position of women is only one aspect of their general concern for unionism. Had less progressive leaders in unions other than these been interviewed, we might have found them less willing to turn their attention to the question of the participation of their women members. Had the women members been from less open unions, we might have found more restiveness, more willingness to see themselves supplanting incumbent leaders.

The male leaders interviewed are busy, follow arduous schedules, and are well aware that their first business is to sustain a cohesive organization capable of a quick, united response in defense of the union's program. Because of their union orientation, they are likely to be less interested in the sex of a union leader than in whether or not the person can handle the job. All believe there is a shortage of able people for the work at hand. The special qualities of discipline combined with assertiveness are difficult to find. If women have these qualities and are willing to give the time required for union work, the leadership indicates it is ready to make room for them. This is more likely to be the case in unions having large numbers of women members or where women are protesting an imbalance in the leadership, for factions weaken the organization and divert it from its basic purpose. A union leader tends to seek solutions to the problems of special groups within the membership. In open unions, the solutions will be those that respond to group needs rather than repress them.

The male leaders of the seven study unions are concerned when they find signs of unhappiness among their women members. They tend to see more problems than the women do in persuading men to accept women in responsible posts. They believe that women usually lack the necessary assertiveness for union work, though not the discipline nor dedication. They envisage problems in finding enough high positions to satisfy both men and women. But they seek to remain flexible. Their hope is that from the ranks of women members sufficient talent will come so that they will be adequately represented, and that they will press for more than tokenism.

144

The words of the women interviewed often appear to
bear out the leaders' judgment that women are not assert-
ive enough. Perhaps the most telling fact is that they do
not easily think of themselves or of any woman as moving
very far up the union leadership ladder. They express
fears of not being able to handle competitive union work,
of lacking toughness. Their experience with male acceptance of women in union roles has led them to think the
men will not object to them provided they know how to
handle the work well. In this they may be too sanguine,
since most have not aimed at the posts filled by men.

The women's principal motivation for union work is
the sense of achievement they derive from accomplishing a
worthwhile task. We do not have data from male rank and
file leaders on this question, but we would expect greater
emphasis from them on the satisfaction derived from being
recognized, since personal ambition is often an important
ingredient of competitiveness. The women's statements and
responses to the attitudinal questionnaire give personal
recognition a low rating. This could be both true and at
the same time self-protective. The women rank and file
leaders appear to be intensely loyal to their unions and
confident that if and when they develop the capacity to
carry heavier responsibility, obstacles will not be put
in their path.

The interviews not only relate the thoughts of men
and women but also point the direction in which women interested in union advancement should move. The way may
be bumpy, but it is not closed. Women must look to themselves if they are to take advantage of opportunities.
They must ready themselves. As they do, they will at the
same time expand those opportunities.

NOTE

1. The New York Times Magazine, March 22, 1970.

OUTLOOK FOR
WOMEN IN UNIONS:
RESEARCH IMPLICATIONS

The introductory chapter of this brief book presented the reader with a general view of women in American labor unions today. Next we focused on the women members of some 108 New York City local unions to see where they fit into the structure of these Locals and what some of the attitudes of the Local officers are toward their participation.

In Chapter 3 the reader was introduced to the seven unions that cooperated closely with us during the year-long investigation. The extent of their cooperation demonstrates the importance to unions of the participation of their members in their labor organizations. It is this involvement and support that spells the difference between life and death for unions in a crisis. Awareness of it is something union leaders carry with them always. To them, it is worth the risk that difficult questions may be asked at union meetings or incumbents sometimes challenged at election time.

In Chapter 4 the rank and file questionnaires from over 1,500 respondents were analyzed to determine the attitudes of both men and women toward participation in their unions. We reflected on some of the problems that must be solved if this activity level is to be substantially increased.

Chapter 5 discussed the views of key leaders interviewed by us and rank and file women leaders interviewed by a specially trained corps of their peers.

In this chapter we hope to relate study findings to some research that has preceded ours in the field of membership participation as well as to look at the implications of our project for labor unions and for future research.

RELATED RESEARCH

While the study reported in this book is the first, to our knowledge, to examine barriers to the participation of women in their labor unions, there have been several studies[1] on membership participation in unions that are useful to review briefly.

Sayles and Strauss[2] studied this subject in 20 local unions over a five-year period, using a definition of participation similar to ours: attending union meetings, voting in union elections, running for local union office, paying union dues, keeping up with union newspapers, filing grievances, and taking part in strikes. Their study, however, focused on groups, because the authors believe that this is the way in which members participate. They found that initial member involvement in the union often began when a shop group saw a particular, perhaps short-run, benefit obtainable through their union if they did become active participants. Success fostered further group participation, leading in turn to such additional benefits as increased political success in the union as well as economic gains. Our study, too, though focused on individuals rather than groups of workers, found that the initial union activity of individuals usually leads to greater commitment, further participation, and the similar benefits of status and accomplishment.

Walker and Guest[3] studied union participation in an auto assembly plant, but their study was of individuals rather than groups. Their findings indicate that workers identify with the union because it provides a sense of belonging. Form and Dansereau[4] report that union members with a social activist orientation to the union participated the most; second most involved were those workers with an economic interest in the union.

In a now-classic study, Rosen and Rosen[5] identified and "named" four groups of union members, and also discovered what our study confirms: that members very much want to be informed about what their union's leaders are doing. The four groups into which they divided union members were the "pickers and choosers," who carefully select where and when to be active and what issues to support; the "patriots," who loyally support the union always; the "gripers," who seem dissatisfied no matter what the union does; and the "fence-sitters," who are often undecided and who tend to answer "don't know" in most studies. The Rosens report that the largest number of members falls into the "pickers and choosers" category; the second largest are "patriots."

It is not hard to assign the "active" and "less active" members in our study into these four groupings: The "actives" tend to be the "patriots"; the "pickers and choosers" are, in our study, the "less actives" who elect to come to union meetings and vote in union elections, though they have not chosen to run for office or serve on a committee. The "gripers" are those who took the time and trouble to write negative comments in the space provided on the questionnaires, and the "fence-sitters" we have already commented upon.

Job satisfaction is coming under increasing scrutiny today, and as early as 1963, Robinson and Connors[6] surveyed several hundred studies on this subject. They reported low (13 percent) job dissatisfaction and high (80 percent) job satisfaction. However, in measuring it, all workers were grouped together, and, as Blauner states,[7] job satisfaction often depends on occupational prestige. Professionals are most satisfied, then higher-level white-collar workers, clericals next, followed by skilled workers and the semiskilled, with unskilled workers having the least satisfaction with their work.

Our study findings on job satisfaction, as discussed in Chapter 3, indicate that occupational prestige is a factor (see meat cutter men, for example) among blue-collar workers, but that other factors play a major role: overqualification for the job performed is an indicator of lower job satisfaction, as is job monotony, impersonality of the work place, and unpleasant or difficult working conditions. Conversely, high job satisfaction is most often found when workers can see the job through from start to finish, or can see the importance of their role in human terms. Blauner's study, referred to earlier, reports a similar finding: that the degree of control over working conditions and the way the job will be done are important determinants of job satisfaction. Pace is especially important. Studies of assembly-line jobs, for example in the automobile industry, indicate that pace may be the biggest problem. Next in importance for auto workers is freedom from direct supervision, then the purposefulness of the job (versus its repetitiveness). Blauner also finds that being a member of a work crew where members have high rapport with one another plays an important role.

Spinrad[8] provides a useful summary of the literature of member participation in unions. He reports that union activists tend to like their jobs, which our findings confirm: The highest percentage of "active" members in our study is satisfied or well-satisfied with their jobs. On the other hand, Spinrad states that workers motivated to job advancement, especially to managerial posts, are less likely to be active; our findings also confirm this, but particularly for men in the union. The reader will recall that it is those men who feel they _cannot_ advance further on their jobs who tend to be most active. The women who felt they _could_ advance were the activists. We suggest as one explanation that women do not see themselves as advancing into managerial posts, but only one or two steps up the job ladder, and view the union as supportive in this limited goal. Very few women interviewed for the study indicated a willingness to move into a job that meant leaving the union and the job security and companionship it provides.

Our findings support Spinrad's conclusion that the union provides vital opportunities for creative participation for workers. The rank and file women leaders interviewed seemed cognizant of this, and their loyalty, even though tempered with certain criticisms, is strong. We found that the women members tend to be, on the average, less critical and more loyal to the union than are the men.

The research work reported by Spinrad provides us with a check list of other factors found to relate to a high degree of union member activity:

- a job in a small plant
- an intimate work community
- a stable work force
- workers free to mingle with one another
- homogeneous work groups
- high status jobs
- urban rather than rural environment
- workers who live and work in the same community
- workers who live close to one another
- union family backgrounds
- friendships with union leaders
- living in working-class neighborhoods rather than middle-class suburbs
- common ethnic ties
- leisure-time associates as fellow workers

Several of these factors relate to the "personal-sociocultural" category of our findings, particularly the desire to know more people at union meetings, and to attend meetings with someone.

Spinrad also finds among active union members a low participation rate in organizations other than their unions, and here again our findings concur.

FURTHER RESEARCH SUGGESTED

With an increasingly automated society and its potential for shorter work weeks and more flexible hours of work, the availability of leisure time and its implications are of major interest to educators and social science researchers alike. The role of labor unions in our society is unique: They relate to the economic lives of their members, provide important social relationships, and offer opportunities for education and self-expression. Much as unions have accomplished in all of these areas, their potential role is even greater. It is with this in mind that we suggest a number of questions for further research.

1. What is the role of social controls on the aspirations of women workers? Research has, until recently, focused primarily on college students or middle-class women. What part do sex-role stereotypes play in the upward mobility of blue-collar women? Are some jobs still considered not feminine by some women? To what extent does the better pay of these jobs offset this? What role does the age of the woman play? Do women still believe they are "taking jobs away from men?" . . . that certain jobs are "too hard for a woman to do?" Does fear of success, so tellingly documented for college women by Matina Horner,[9] play as large a role in the lives of blue-collar women?

2. Several major unions have established Women's Departments to encourage participation of women members and to assist in focusing on their concerns. How do these departments increase the awareness of women? For example, how has coverage of news relating to women members and use of the union's "Women's Page" changed since introduction of these departments in unions? No comparative study has yet been done of Women's Departments, programs, and methods they are utilizing, nor of their achievements. One union, the International Union of Electrical Workers, has conducted three self-surveys of offices held by women members to determine which posts and how many are held by women and whether the Social Action and Women's Activities Committees of the union are effective in stimulating women to run for union office and hold committee jobs. Results

150

so far seem encouraging, the union reports. Six years ago
Alice Cook wrote:

> Union leaders, however, are more often
> than not uneasy about the political self-
> consciousness among women members which
> such a department generates when it is
> successful. But to the extent that it
> can and often does confine women's ac-
> tivities within its limits, there to ven-
> tilate and exhaust their grievances the
> device is probably a least-cost answer to
> increasing women's participation in union
> affairs without risking serious challenge
> to traditional male hegemony.[10]

Testing the validity of this statement today should be
both valuable and interesting.

3. The "active" union women in our study were most
often those who were single or formerly married, and the
sole support of their families. How do they manage their
time? How do they accommodate their extra responsibilities and make room for union activities? It would be useful to learn not only how they are able to manage, but
what kinds of services would ease their lives.[11] Students
discussing this subject in a Cornell labor extension class
for union women indicated that for most of them union activity meant cutting back on sleep. (The amount of sleep
each student averaged per night ranged from four to six
and a half hours.)

4. Several researchers in the past have found a reluctance on the part of workers to file grievances, con-
cluding that it is an admission of a need for assistance
that workers would rather go without than admit. Our
findings indicate generally a low use of grievance procedure. Does this indicate low success in resolving grievances? Or do other factors account for it? Further research could examine how workers perceive grievance procedure, why they might be reluctant to sign a written
grievance form, whether they fear punishment by management
if they file formal grievances, and if indeed, this fear
is justified. How do the attitudes of men and women differ in perception and use of grievance procedures? What
can unions do, if it seems necessary, to further dignify
grievance procedure? Where there is no reluctance to
utilize grievance procedures, what conditions prevail to
make this the case?

5. Are the study findings reported in this book pecu-
liar to urban working women in labor unions, or are they
more universally applicable? Replication of this study is
suggested for semirural and suburban environments and for
smaller cities than New York, utilizing different unions
and industries as well as different Locals of our study
unions. We need to know more about the attitudes of men
and women in the important mass-production industries, and
how union participation in other occupations compares with
that represented in our study. What barriers are the same
as those uncovered in our study, and what new ones are of
significance?

6. "Active" union women perceive their supervisors
as especially hard on them. This differs from the percep-
tions of men and "less active" women members. What is the
reality? If supervisors are resentful of women who are
more active in their unions, what can be done to modify
these attitudes? Is there a role for union representatives in achieving this attitude change? Would steward-
ship courses in grievance handling, which incorporate role
playing or other simulation exercises, help women deal
more effectively with hostility from supervisors?

7. Study findings indicate that when grievance procedure is used, it is used more by women than men. Is
there a pattern to these grievances? Are they based on
plant conditions that reflect the kinds of jobs women tend
to hold, or are they sex related? Are women blocked in
getting their grievances solved? If so, how? What kinds
of women's grievances tend to utilize all the steps
through arbitration? Do they differ in substance or pro-
cessing from men's grievances that follow the same route?

8. Have the Equal Pay Act and Title VII of the Civil
Rights Act made significant differences in the kinds of
grievances initiated, and in those that go to arbitration?
A comparative analysis of cases in the period 1955-65 and
1965-75 would be useful.

9. Part-time work is on the increase, and so is the
demand for part-time jobs. There will be increasing problems of integrating part-time workers into the life of
unions. How do they view their unions? What are the attitudes of full-time workers toward the part-time work
force? Of union staff? Of management? How can unions
reach part-time workers more effectively? Extensive attitudinal research coupled with program follow-up is suggested.

10. Women seem to have accepted the role allocated to
them both in the work force and in the union. What in the

socialization process provides the basis for this acceptance? Can this be traced with any precision? Attitudes
of women workers are changing. To what is this attributable? What is the effect of the rising education among
all workers? More and more of the younger workers, both
men and women, have had working mothers as family role
models before they themselves enter the work force. What
part does this play in attitude change? Government en-
forcement of equal employment opportunity law, the women's
movement, and increased visibility of women in the press
and on television, all are factors. To what extent?
There has been much speculation but little documented research into the reasons for attitude changes among women
in the work force.

     11. Except in the questionnaire choice, "My husband
would have to agree to my being active in the union," and
in the interviews of rank and file leaders by women who
were their peers, there was no attempt in this study to
examine how attitudes of family members affect participation of women in labor unions. What is the relation between a husband's attitude toward his wife's working, and
her role in the union to which she belongs? A survey by
McCall's magazine, reported in its June 1974 issue, suggests that the more dependent the family is on the wife's
earnings, the less the husband tends to approve of her
holding a job outside the home. Is income more a deter-
minant of attitude than age, for example? If younger
couples have, in fact, different attitudes toward a woman's participation as worker and unionist than middle-aged
or older couples, what is likely to be the long-run effect?
Does a husband's attitude differ toward his wife's participation in church, PTA, or community groups? And if so,
why?

IMPLICATIONS OF STUDY FINDINGS COMMON
TO THE SEVEN UNIONS

     Certain study findings common to all seven unions
raise problems and opportunities which unions either are
presently considering or will need to take up in the near
future.
     1. One of the universal needs is to involve younger
members, both men and women, in the union. Men and women
active in their unions tend to be over 45 years of age.
This is true of 65 percent of the male respondents and 70
percent of the female. An even higher percentage of shop

stewards are over 45: 66 percent of the men, 77 of the women. This rises again when the ages of women elected to office are examined: 80 percent are over 45. This is considerably higher than the proportion of women over 45 in the study (66 percent). On the other hand, when we look at the percentage of men over 45 elected to office, we find that it is exactly that of those in the study population—43 percent. Activating younger women at every level is important to all seven unions.

2. Members in all the unions wanted more information about the union if they were to become more active, and to know why it mattered to the union whether or not they participated. One in every three less active members feels this way. Yet each of the unions has a newspaper designed to reach its membership and keep it informed, plus a shop steward or delegate system and paid business representatives, all with this goal in mind. What then are the most relevant channels for communicating? Where are they breaking down? What can be done about it? What kinds of information do members want that they do not presently receive? How involved are the members themselves in the process of communicating: Is it a two-way interchange?

3. The question of when and where to hold union meetings for maximum attendance continues to plague all unions. Night meetings in an urban environment present particular obstacles, in addition to excluding night shift workers. Availability of transportation as well as its cost accentuates this difficulty. Child care poses added problems.

4. Member comments on questionnaires indicate that revamping meetings to make them more interesting and to provide a greater role in them for the individual are important considerations for unions. Women especially voice feelings that they are not listened to at meetings, that what they think on issues does not really matter to the union.

5. In each union we found a high number of requests both for education programs and for leadership training. This was especially true for women members, and overwhelmingly so in those unions with a high proportion of minority women.

6. A uniform response that leaders in the seven unions found hard to account for was that active union women thought supervisors were hard on them. Almost one in three active union women felt this way. It seems to point up the experience-skill gap that causes many women

to feel ill-equipped to deal with this management response. It provides good reason for steward training programs that, together with grievance handling, incorporate some emphasis on how to deal with supervisor hostility.

7. In each study union there seems to be a pool of 15 to 20 percent of the membership not now active who have nothing standing in the way of their increased activity. How to reach and involve this group constitutes an important question.

8. The study showed that in each of the unions, there was a need for attitude change, both on the part of women in their feelings about themselves and their role in the union, and on the part of men in their acceptance of women in new roles. From women in each union came suggestions such as have more women as guest speakers at union meetings to show both men and women that women are leaders, appoint more women to staff positions, pay more attention to what women say at meetings, urge male staff members to set the example for other men in the union in treating women members as equals, hold courses for women members, especially courses such as public speaking and parliamentary procedure, grievance handling, and collective bargaining.

9. We found a significant difference in all seven unions in the way leaders define "interested in the union" and the way women members define it. The women believe they are "interested" if they attend meetings, vote in union elections, and give overall support to their union. Leaders tend to define "interested" as accepting responsibility, holding committee posts, or running for office. In each union most of the women who moved from the member definition to the leader definition did so as a result of individual encouragement, usually from union leaders. Therefore, if unions seek the increased participation of their women members and their acceptance of additional responsibilities, these members will have to feel necessary to their union, be asked to help, see a role they can play, and receive the training and encouragement that enable them to gain confidence and go on to even further participation.

TRADE UNION WOMEN'S STUDIES PROGRAM

How to find and develop leaders, especially among younger members and women, is an area of major union concern expressed in all leader interviews. Each of the

155

unions looks to its own membership as the ultimate source
for paid union staff, when there are openings, as well as
of rank and file leaders. It is because this union concern for developing leaders combines with the strong desire of union women for education, leadership training,
and a larger role in their unions that we have embarked
on an extensive Trade Union Women's Studies program.

Following our year-long study, and with the advice of
an enlarged trade union advisory committee, we have embarked on a long-range leadership training and labor
studies program for trade union women. This was made
possible through a new grant from the Ford Foundation.
Initially, a series of five short courses was developed
to reach out to union women. Special materials were prepared: on tool subjects--grievance handling and effective speaking; in content areas--working women and the
law and women in the work force today; and a background
course on women in American labor history. We offered
these to women unionists through Cornell's New York office and also through individual unions, where we tailored
the courses to meet the needs and structures of those organizations.

This was the first step in what is viewed as an education and leadership training ladder for union women.
It leads to a year-long college credit program with
courses geared specifically to developing skills and in-
sights of women unionists. The first year of credit
courses includes:

> Writing and Study Skills
> The Anatomy of a Contract
> Oral Communications and Logic
> Women in American Labor History
> Psychology of Leadership
> Women's Role in Union Organization and
>   Administration

Special tutorial services are available to students
to brush up on writing, research, and study skills. Two
special features of the program are a morning session for
night shift workers and those who work Saturday but have
a day off during the week and an evening session commenc-
ing an hour earlier than Cornell's usual classes--at five
instead of six in the evening--with lost time, if students
incur it, reimbursed up to one hour. We are testing
whether there is sufficient need for released time for
education to make it useful as a collective bargaining
demand.

As a regular part of this education ladder, students will have the opportunity to join the second year of an ongoing two-year Cornell Labor/Liberal Arts program, receiving a special certificate in labor studies upon completion. Interested students will be encouraged to continue to work for an Associate in the Arts or a Bachelor of Arts degree, and they will receive college credit toward this for their work in the Labor/Liberal Arts program.

The Trade Union Women's Studies program will be offered by Cornell ILR Extension in other cities of New York State, linking us up with Community Colleges and branches of the State University. Thus, new opportunities in adult education will be opened to trade union women. Programs in Buffalo and Rochester are already underway.

The heart of the program of Trade Union Women's Studies is, however, its day-to-day work with union women through their labor organizations. For example, a monthly seminar of union women leaders and staff, meeting regularly under Cornell sponsorship, planned and held a major citywide conference for union women. On an icy day in January 1974, over 600 women unionists and a scattering of men from 104 Locals and 48 international unions met to discuss some special concerns of working women: affirmative action on the job, organizing unorganized women workers, increasing participation of women in unions, and collective bargaining issues which incorporated women's needs.

The Trade Union Women's Studies program also sponsors conferences on special topics and publishes proceedings from these to augment their usefulness. The development of a substantial Materials Center on working women is an integral part of this program and includes books, periodicals, and an extensive up-to-date clipping file. It is utilized by union and university students, faculty, and independent researchers.

A second study by the authors, longitudinal in nature, is planned for the Trade Union Women's Studies education ladder described above. It will assess the practical value of this program of labor education and leadership training in helping women become more involved in the life of their trade unions.

CONCLUSIONS

In this chapter we have examined related research on the participation of members in their unions and suggested several areas where further research might be fruitful. Some implications for labor unions in the study findings

157

have been set forth, and one follow-up program, the Trade
Union Women's Studies of the New York State School of Industrial and Labor Relations, Cornell University, has been
described. The value of this program to the individual
trade union women who participate in it and, through them,
to their unions is being measured and will be reported in
the future.

Sayles and Strauss, in the epilogue to their book,
conclude that unions have lost much of their earlier ideal-
istic momentum and will have difficulty in finding new
blood. "Now there are fewer men [sic] of this sort among
the ranks, and many of the best are offered management
positions as soon as they show ability as union officers."[1]

It is now some 12 years later. We suggest it is time
unions look to their women members for some of this leadership. We find among women unionists a vitality of spirit
and a verve reminiscent of the union spirit of the 1930s
and 1940s. There is a crusading zeal, especially for the
task of organizing the 25 million unorganized women workers
in factories, stores, hospitals, and offices throughout
this land.

We have found women union members devoted and dedicated. We have found them able and tireless. They believe in labor unions and want to work within and through
their unions to help--for they are helpers--and to lead--
for they are leaders--in carrying the labor movement forward to new levels of achievement that will mean a better
life for all Americans.

NOTES

1. For several valuable references we are indebted
to Edward Gross, Industry and Social Life (Dubuque, Iowa:
William C. Brown Co., 1965).
2. Leonard Sayles and George Strauss, The Local
Union, rev. ed. (New York: Harcourt, Brace and World,
Inc., 1967), pp. 107-23.
3. C. R. Walker and R. H. Guest, The Man on the
Assembly Line (Cambridge, Mass.: Harvard University
Press, 1952).
4. W. H. Form and H. K. Dansereau, "Union Member
Orientations and Patterns of Social Integration," Industrial and Labor Relations Review 11 (1957): 3-12.
5. Hjalmar Rosen and R. A. Hudson Rosen, The Union
Member Speaks (Englewood Cliffs, N.J.: Prentice-Hall,
1955).

6. H. A. Robinson and R. P. Connors, "Job Satisfaction Researches of 1962," The Personnel and Guidance Journal 42 (1963): 136-42.

7. Robert Blauner, "Work Satisfaction in Modern Society," Contemporary Labor Issues (Belmont, Calif.: Wadsworth Publishing Co., 1968).

8. William Spinrad, "Correlates of Trade Union Participation: A Summary of the Literature," American Sociological Review 25, no. 2 (April 1960): 237-44.

9. Matina Horner, "Toward an Understanding of Achievement--Related Conflicts in Women," Journal of Social Issues 28, no. 2 (1972): 157.

10. Alice Cook, "Women and American Trade Unions," Annals of the American Academy (January 1968): 130-31.

11. For 16 months in 1972-73 Alice Cook, Professor Emeritus of the School of Industrial and Labor Relations, Cornell University, traveled to Europe, the Middle East, and Asia to study urban married women in the work force in some 10 countries. Comparative research in urban centers of the United States, using the same questions she asked her respondents (for example, "How do you manage?" and "What services would make your life easier?"), is suggested as of special interest.

12. Sayles and Strauss, op. cit., p. 159.

THE SURVEY METHODS AND PROCEDURES

Three instruments were used to collect the data for the study: (1) a questionnaire designed to provide an overview of the participation of women members of New York City local unions having substantial numbers of women members; (2) a questionnaire distributed to rank and file members of seven New York local unions that focused on reasons for the varied levels of activity of the women members (see Appendix C); (3) an attitudinal questionnaire administered to rank and file women leaders in these seven cooperating local unions (see Appendix D).

Information gathered from these sources was supplemented by interviews with officers and other leaders of the seven unions and by examination of union documents. An Advisory Committee of trade union leaders and university faculty and staff aided in the design of the study and interpretation of its results.

ADVISORY COMMITTEE

Central to the study was the guidance and direction provided by its Advisory Committee. The committee met at the outset of the project to review its purposes and methods for gathering data. The accumulated experience and the active involvement of Advisory Committee members were invaluable to the conduct of the study. A complete listing of the members appears in Appendix B.

QUESTIONNAIRE TO NEW YORK CITY LOCAL UNIONS

The listing by the U.S. Department of Labor of the relative proportions of male and female members of international unions was used as the basis for the initial selection of New York City local unions to receive what we termed the "overview" questionnaire. The data of this questionnaire would be used to define the typical level of participation of women union members when their number was a significant proportion of the union's total membership. Local unions of parent internationals reporting

30 percent or more of their national membership as female were identified through the New York State Directory of Labor Organizations and the Directory of Affiliates of the New York City Central Labor Council, AFL-CIO. Our initial identification gave us 322 local unions.

An explanatory letter outlining the purpose and design of the study was sent to the chief officer of each of these local unions, together with a questionnaire seeking information about the activity of their women members, their opinions on the reasons for the levels of activity they observed, and some information about the kinds of jobs the women hold in the industries covered by these unions. The New York City Central Labor Council, AFL-CIO, endorsing this study, recommended to its affiliates that they cooperate in returning questionnaires, and an editorial appeared in the Labor Chronicle, official publication of the City Central Labor Council, to this effect.

Responses to the letters and questionnaires, together with further recovery efforts, were used to eliminate those Locals that did not have large numbers of women members even though their international unions did. The initial identification was reduced to a total of 238 local unions. Of these, 103 questionnaires were returned on behalf of 111 local unions. This represents a 46.6-percent response. Questionnaires were distributed and collected during November and December 1972, and January and February 1973.

QUESTIONNAIRE TO RANK AND FILE MEMBERS

In order to identify barriers to the participation of women in the activities of their unions, a questionnaire was drafted for circulation to the rank and file members of the seven local unions cooperating in the second phase of the study. The draft was reviewed by the Advisory Committee and other leaders of the seven unions, pretested, and redesigned for final distribution to both men and women members of these Locals.

Certain modifications were made at the request of the Meat Cutters', Local 342, and the "New York Metro Area (Postal Union)" in the questionnaires distributed to their members. Question 11, "Could you advance or be upgraded from the job you now hold?" was omitted for the Meat Cutters'. Question 4, "National or Racial Origin (optional)" was omitted for the "New York Metro Area (Postal Union)." Since several of the unions have a

large number of Hispanic members, questionnaires were
printed in both Spanish and English except for the Store
Workers' and the Postal Union.

In order to ensure the maximum membership response
and to underscore the full cooperation of the local union
in the survey, questionnaires were distributed through the
unions themselves. In most cases, one of the directors of
the study met with the shop stewards or business agents at
special meetings called by the unions, and the purpose of
the study was explained. Its importance was emphasized by
the union's president or key officer, and publicized in
the Local's newspaper. Instructions were given on dis-
tributing the questionnaires in a random pattern, and the
stewards or business agents were requested to collect the
returns and forward them to the New York City office of
the School of Industrial and Labor Relations in the post-
paid enveloped provided. In one case, the president preferred to mail the questionnaires to all members, together
with a letter from him and return envelope to the project
office.

The method of distribution ensured involvement of the
union but risked returns from somewhat more active members
than would be representative for the union as a whole. To
guard against undue skewing of the results, the returned
questionnaires were sorted into "active" and "less active"
categories, using question 13 as the index of activity.
The responses of these two groups to other questions were
examined separately to permit identification of the opinions and characteristics of each group. A total of 5,650
questionnaires were distributed and 1,373 questionnaires
returned, representing a 24-percent response. The number
of invalid questionnaires was 186, reducing the population
studied to 1,188.

One object of the study was to reflect the positions
of women as distinct from those of men, while at the same
time retaining an undistorted representation of the responses characteristic of each union as a whole. To
achieve this object, male and female returns were weighted
to represent the proportions of men and women in each
union. The weighted population studied was 1,516. Two
sets of returns, those from International Ladies' Garment
Workers' Union Local 22 and from the University Hospital
members of District 1199, were so overwhelmingly female
(approximately 90 percent) that only questionnaires of
women members were examined.

Questionnaires were distributed and collected during
the months of November and December 1972.

INTERVIEWS AND SUPPLEMENTARY
ATTITUDINAL QUESTIONNAIRE

A total of 39 rank and file women leaders were interviewed by 12 of their peers. The interviewers were trained
in interviewing skills through a day-long workshop (see Appendix E). These women, representing each of the seven
local unions cooperating in the second phase of the study,
interviewed women belonging to one of these seven unions--
but different from their own. Interviews were conducted
in January and February of 1974.

Each of those interviewed also completed an attitudinal questionnaire adapted from the "Work Values Questionnaire" used by Helen Bickel Wolfe[1] in her expansion of
Lorraine D. Eyde's[2] study of the work values of college
women. It was necessary to create a new category to measure the value of union work and to omit the economic
value included in measures of other work. The items in
the questionnaire sets represent six work values:
dominance-recognition, independence, interesting activity, loyalty-dependence, mastery-achievement, and social.
Respondents rank-ordered their responses to the forced
choice of each set of each of the six values.

Interviews were also conducted with leading officers
of the seven unions in Phase II of the study. These interviews, conducted by the authors, included the president
of each local union and at least two other key officers or
staff members. In addition, the survey findings were reported to these leaders, and their interpretation was
solicited. In all, 44 key officers and staff members
were interviewed. In every case where a woman held that
position, she was included.

LIMITATIONS OF THE STUDY

No attempt was made to do a thorough study of the
local unions in New York City having substantial numbers
of women members. Instead, the aim was, by means of a
brief questionnaire, to compile the views of those leaders and a description of the participation level of the
women in their union. Almost half of the unions identified responded. The overview summary appearing in Chapter 2 represents only the situation of those unions.

The selection of seven unions for the more intensive
focus of Phase II of the study does not constitute a
stratification of New York City unions representing

industries that employ large numbers of women. It does, however, yield representative information on seven industries that do employ large numbers of women. Two from the public sector were chosen to represent federal and municipal portions of that sector.

Questionnaire returns from the Phase I overview survey of leaders and from the Phase II survey of rank and file members must be interpreted as more likely to depict the views of unions, leaders, and members who have more than an ordinary interest in the primary question of this survey: barriers to the participation of women in local labor unions.

A study of this dimension must be viewed in the framework of action research, which it is, rather than pure research, which it is not. No attempt was made to be exhaustive. We hoped to accumulate data that would help in formulating a workers' education program for labor union women, based on their needs and directed toward increasing their participation in their union organizations. The findings of this exploratory research did, indeed, indicate areas where some of the needs expressed by the unions and their members lend themselves to possible remedy through a variety of education programs.

NOTES

1. Helen Bickel Wolf, "Women in the World of Work," State University of New York, The State Education Department, Division of Research, Albany, N.Y., 1969.

2. Lorraine D. Eyde, "Work Values and Background Factors as Productors of Women's Desire to Work," Research Monograph No. 108, Bureau of Business Research, Ohio State University, 1962.

ADVISORY COMMITTEE TO THE STUDY OF LABOR UNION WOMEN

Nickolas Abondolo
President
Local 342, Amalgamated Meat
Cutters and Retail Food Store
Employees

Julius Berry
Labor Program Specialist
Metropolitan Office, NYSSILR

Morris Biller
President
New York Metropolitan Area
Postal Union

Marie Calera
Manager, Complaints Department
Dress Joint Council, Local 22,
International Ladies' Garment
Workers' Union

Jennie Farley
Assistant Professor
Cornell University

Lois Gray
Assistant Dean, NYSSILR
Cornell University
Director, Metropolitan Office

Gloria Johnson
Director
Education and Women's Activities,
International Union of Electrical
Workers

Betty Goetz Lall
Director
Union/University Urban Affairs
Program, Metropolitan Office,
NYSSILR

Annie B. Martin
Assistant Industrial Commissioner
State of New York, Department of
Labor

Lillian Roberts
Associate Director
District Council 37, AFSCME

Eleanor Tilson
Administrator
Security Plan, United Department
Store Workers' Union

John Toto
Director
White-Collar Division
District Council 37, American
Federation of State, County, and
Municipal Employees

James Trenz
President
Local 463, IUE

Doris Turner
Secretary
National Union of Hospital and
Health Care Employees

QUESTIONNAIRE TO RANK AND FILE MEMBERS OF SEVEN LOCAL UNIONS

Questionnaire to Union Members on Why They Are or Are Not
Active in Their Unions

Please return to: NYSSILR, Cornell University, 7 East 43 Street, New York,
N.Y. 10017.

Our local is cooperating in a survey of men and women in unions.
Will you help by taking a few minutes to fill out this questionnaire?
There is no need to sign your name. Thank you.

Please do not
write below.

GENERAL INFORMATION

1. Sex   2. Age   3. Married status

    ☐ Man   ☐ Under 25   ☐ Married

    ☐ Woman   ☐ 25 - 35   ☐ Divorced, Separa-
                                                    ted, Widowed,
                           ☐ 35 - 45   etc.

                           ☐ Over 45

4. National or Racial Origin (optional)_____

5. Children How many children, if any, do you have?_____
              What are their ages?_____

6. Education What is the last year of schooling you
               completed?_____
               Are you currently enrolled in any courses?_____

7. Are you the sole support of your household?_____

WORK SITUATION

8. Have you -- ? (please check one)

    ☐ 1. Just recently begun to work?

    ☐ 2. Worked, stopped for children, returned to work?

    ☐ 3. Worked, stopped for other reasons, returned to work?

    ☐ 4. Always worked?

9. Exactly what is your job?_____
    Is this -- ? (check one) __
                              __ 1. Full-time __ 2. Part-time

166

. How satisfied are you with the <u>job</u> itself? (check one)

☐ 1. Dislike it   ☐ 4. Well satisfied

☐ 2. Slightly dissatisfied   ☐ 5. Enjoy it

☐ 3. Satisfied

. Could you advance or be upgraded from the job you now hold?

☐ 1. Yes   ☐ 2. No   ☐ 3. Not sure

ION PARTICIPATION

2. How long have you been a member of your union?_____

3. Have you ever -- ? (check all that you have done)

☐ 1. Used the grievance procedure

☐ 2. Attended a membership meeting

☐ 3. Attended a social event sponsored by the union

☐ 4. Attended an educational program of the union

☐ 5. Voted in a union election

☐ 6. Been a committee member

☐ 7. Been a shop steward, delegate, or shop chairman

☐ 8. Been chairman of a committee

☐ 9. Run for a union office

☐ 10. Been elected to an office

OMMENTS

4. What would have to change in your life to make it easier for
you to participate in union affairs? (check as many as you
want)
A. <u>Personal</u>

☐ 1. Nothing would have to change   ☐ 4. Fewer activities
                                         in other groups
☐ 2. Fewer home responsibilities   I like

☐ 3. More information about union   ☐ 5. Would need to
                                         speak better
                                         English

167

☐ 6. Would need to feel more competent

☐ 7. Would want to go to meetings with someone

☐ 8. Would want to know more people who would be at the meetings

☐ 9. My husband or wife would have to agree to my being active in the union

☐ 10. I am a woman and think men are better at union affairs

☐ 11. I am just not interested in union affairs

☐ 12. Other _____
_____

B. <u>Job</u> Are there things about your job that affect your being active in the union? (check as many as you want)

☐ 1. Supervisor should not make life hard for active unionists

☐ 2. Union activity would have to give me a better chance to get ahead on the job

☐ 3. I would need to work on another shift

☐ 4. I work part-time and the union doesn't affect me much

☐ 5. People who hold important jobs in the shop deserve union positions

☐ 6. People who have been here longer should run the union

☐ 7. Nothing about the job affects my union activity

☐ 8. Other_____

C. <u>Union</u> What could the union do to make it easier for you to participate? (check as many as you want)

☐ 1. Meetings would have to be held in more convenient place

☐ 2. Meetings should be at a different time for me

☐ 3. I would need some child care arrangements in order to come to meetings

☐ 4. Union should encourage me to be active

168

☐ 5. I would like to know more about what is accomplished in the union by people like me

☐ 6. I would be interested in union social events

☐ 7. I would like educational programs

☐ 8. I would like to learn some of the things a person needs to be a leader

☐ 9. Union leaders need to give more recognition to people who do union work

☐ 10. Union does not need to do anything more

☐ 11. Other_____

Do you think more women should run for union office? (please check one)

☐ Yes   ☐ No   ☐ Not sure

Do you think women generally take as much interest in the union as men?

☐ Yes   ☐ No   ☐ Not sure

THANK YOU FOR YOUR HELP

MOTIVATIONS FOR UNION WORK

Metropolitan Office, New York State School of Industrial and Labor
Relations, Cornell University, 7 East 43 Street, New York, N.Y. 100~

Listed below are some reasons why people are active in unions. Plea
rate the reasons in each group according to their importance to you,
using the numbers 1 through 6.

Mark 1 for the reason that fits you best in each group. Rate the
others in the order of their importance until you mark 6 for the
reason that is least important of all.

For example: _1_ most important reason for you
              _2_ next most important
              _3_ somewhat important
              _4_ less important
              _5_ not particularly important
              _6_ least important of all

There is no need to sign this. Just put it in the attached envelope
and mail it.

I am active in the union because I want to...

A.
___ keep busy
___ make myself heard
___ develop myself
___ not be bossed by others
___ be with other people
___ be cooperative

B.
___ keep alert
___ be recognized
___ be obliging
___ do things my own way
___ feel that life is not dull
___ make friends

C.
___ be independent
___ influence people
___ have new experiences
___ get to know people
___ help out the union office
___ improve all the time

D.
___ tell the boss what to do
___ avoid being told what to do
___ do what is expected of me
___ be able to talk about someth:
    besides the usual
___ be helpful to others
___ avoid being lonely

E.
___ have people like me
___ get something done
___ avoid dull work
___ carry out union policies
___ make decisions for myself
___ tell others what to do

F.
___ be part of the team
___ use my training and educatior
___ show others how to do things
___ know different people
___ depend more on myself
___ do something interesting

G.
___ have different experiences
___ show my loyalty
___ assist fellow workers
___ stand up for myself
___ feel valued
___ get out more

170

RANK AND FILE WOMEN LEADERS WHO
INTERVIEWED FOR THE STUIY

Mary Bell, Custodial Assistants, District Council 37
  AFSCME

Bernice Cattrell, Local 463, IUE

Joy Donato, Local 342, Meat Cutters and Retail Food Store
  Employees

Louise Evans, Hospital Workers, District 1199

Anne Godfrey, Department Store Workers, Local 2

Janet Hornedo, Department Store Workers, Local 3

Ruth Jaysura, Postal Union

Laura Rodriguez, Local 22, ILGWU

Emily Sterrett, Local 22, ILGWU

Wilma Strudwick, Local 463, IUE

Maryama Wadood, Postal Union

Marian Whitmore, Local 342, Meat Cutters and Retail Food
  Store Employees

workers in, 44-45; women's participation in, 44

American Federation of State, County and Municipal Employees (District Council 37, Custodial Assistants Local 1597), 19, 37; characteristics of District Council, 49-51; characteristics of local, 51-53; women's participation in, 52-53

American Postal Workers Union AFL-CIO, 40

Bailey, Eleanor, 40
barriers to participation in unions, 19, 90-108
Bell, Mary, 171
Berry, Julius, 165
Biller, Morris (Moe), 40, 165
Blauner, Robert, 159
Bowyer, Matthew, 82
Breslow, Israel, 63, 132
business agents, number of women serving as, 28

CIO. See Congress of Industrial Organizations
CLUW. See Coalition of Labor Union Women
Calera, Marie, 62, 63, 165
Callahan, Mary, 46
Cattrell, Bernice, 48, 171
children, effect of on mothers' participation in union, 137-138
Coalition of Labor Union Women, founding of, 11
competency of women officers, union officials' views of, 121-123
Congress of Industrial Organizations, 54
Connors, R. P., 159
Cook, Alice H., 17, 159

Cornell University School of Industrial and Labor Relations, education programs, 42, 157-158
Crumedy, John, 51, 123, 127-128
cultural barriers for women in unions, 19
Custodial Assistants. See American Federation of State, County and Municipal Employees

Dansereau, H. K., 158
Davis, Leon, 58, 59, 124, 125
demographic characteristics of holders and non-holders of offices, 114-120
Domanico, Joanna, 58
Donato, Joy, 171
Drug and Hospital Employees' Union (District 1199), 19. See also National Union of Hospital and Health Care Employees (District 1199)

earnings of women compared to men, 2, 6-7
education programs, Amalgamated Meat Cutters' and Retail Food Store Employees' Union (Local 342), 42-43; Cornell University School of Industrial and Labor Relations, 42, 157-158; leadership courses for women, 155-157; National Union of Hospital and Health Care Employees (District 1199), 58; in survey unions, 24-25; women's participation in, 86, 88
educational level of union members, 66
employment of women, reasons for, 2

of on union participation by women, 85-120; opinions of on women seeking office, 108, 110; personal and sociocultural reasons for low participation, 90-98; questionnaires sent to, 161-162, 166-169; resistance to women's leadership, 143; sole support status, 69; types of, 147-148; union-related reasons for low participation, 101-108; work histories, 70; see also activists in unions; leaders of unions

members of unions (men), attitudes toward women's participation, 130-132; see also activists in unions (men); leaders of unions (men)

members of unions (women), causes for low participation, 32; characteristics of in New York City, 13; education programs for leadership development, 155-157; relationship of number of to number of women leaders, 29, 30-31. See also activists in unions (women); leaders of unions (women); Work force (women)

men in unions. See activists in unions (men); leaders of unions (men); members of unions (men)

Michelson, William, 54, 123, 126

minority group workers, proportion of women, 13

Mirsky, Rose, 63

motivation, of women active in unions, 138-143, 170; of women officers, 123-126

NALC. See National Association of Letter Carriers

Nash, Al, 83

National Association of Letter Carriers, 39

National Union of Hospital and Health Care Employees (District 1199), 37; characteristics of, 56-60; women's participation in, 58, 59-60

New York City, number of trade union women, 13; number of women workers, 13; racial proportion of women workers, 13

New York City local unions, characteristics of those surveyed, 22-25; questionnaires sent to heads of, 160-161; survey of, 21-22. See also survey unions

New York Metro Area Postal Union, 18, 37; characteristics of, 38-41; women members' problems, 41; women's participation in, 40

Newman, Pauline, 60

officers of unions. See leaders of unions

participants in unions. See activists in unions; leaders of unions

participation in unions. See entries under activists in unions; leaders of unions; members of unions, etc.

Perlow, Austin, 82

personal barriers for participation in unions, 19, 90-98

position holders in unions. See leaders of unions

United Store Workers' Union
(Locals 2 and 3), 19, 37;
characteristics of, 53-56;
women's participation in,
54-56
upgrading programs. See
education programs

Van Arsdale, Harry, Jr., 13

Wadood, Maryama, 171
Walker, C. R., 158
Whitmore, Marian, 171
Wolf, Helen Bickel, 164
women, life expectancy of, 1
women in unions. See activists in unions (women);
leaders of unions (women);
members of unions (women)
women's movement, effect of
on trade union women, 11-13
work force (women), characteristics of in New York
City, 13; size of, 1-2;
women's reasons for joining, 2. See also members
of unions (women)
work histories of union members, 70
Wyatt, Addie, 11

Zimmerman, Charles, 63

BARBARA M. WERTHEIMER is Director of Trade Union Women's Studies, a program for developing labor studies and leadership training programs for union women. She formerly served as consultant for the New York State Division of Housing and Community Renewal, and has also headed the National Education Department of the Amalgamated Clothing Workers.

Ms. Wertheimer is author of <u>Exploring the Arts: A Handbook for Trade Union Program Planners</u>, as well as numerous other adult and worker education publications. She is currently at work on the forthcoming <u>We Were There, the Story of Working Women in America</u>.

Ms. Wertheimer has a B.A. degree from Oberlin College and an M.A. from New York University.

ANNE H. NELSON is Associate Director of Trade Union Women's Studies and specializes in questions of working women's relations with the economy and with organized labor. Formerly, she served as a research and planning consultant for Nelson Associates.

Ms. Nelson has published <u>The Visible Union in Times of Stress: A Study of the Union Counseling Program of the New York City Central Labor Council</u>, and is co-author of <u>Public Library Systems in the United States</u>.

Anne Nelson has a B.A. in economics from Oberlin College.

WOMEN IN ACADEMIA: Evolving Policies Toward
Equal Opportunities
    Edited by Arie Y. Lewin, Elga Wasserman,
    and Linda Bleiweis

THE SCOPE OF BARGAINING IN PUBLIC EMPLOYMENT
    Joan Weitzman

THE AGING WORKER AND THE UNION: Employment and
Retirement of Middle-Aged and Older Workers
    Ewan Clague, Balraj Palli, and Leo Kramer

REFORM IN TRADE UNION DISCRIMINATION IN THE
CONSTRUCTION INDUSTRY: Operation Dig and Its Legacy
    Irwin Dubinsky

INTERNATIONAL MANUAL ON COLLECTIVE BARGAINING FOR
PUBLIC EMPLOYEES
    Edited by Seymour P. Kaye and Arthur Marsh

WORK OR WELFARE? Factors in the Choice for
AFDC Mothers
    Mildred Rein